3

Trevor Watt

Union Theol Sem
New York.

Feb 11, 1961

A Layman's Guide to Protestant Theology

THE MACMILLAN COMPANY
NEW YORK • CHICAGO
DALLAS • ATLANTA • SAN FRANCISCO
LONDON • MANILA
IN CANADA
BRETT-MACMILLAN LTD.
GALT, ONTARIO

A Layman's Guide to Protestant Theology

WILLIAM HORDERN

New York 1960
THE MACMILLAN COMPANY

Printed in the United States of America

Ninth Printing 1960

To My Wife

Acknowledgments

In a book of this nature, it is impossible to make adequate acknowledgment of all the sources that one has used. Inasmuch as I am trying to interpret theology for the lay or non-technical reader, I feel that extensive footnotes would be a hindrance. The section "Suggestions for Further Reading" is in no way a complete bibliography of the sources upon which I have drawn. It is a compilation of works that I believe will interest the layman. I am, of course, indebted to a host of authors too numerous to mention here.

A word of special gratitude must be expressed to William Hubben, editor of *Friends Intelligencer.* Early in 1953 he asked me to write a series of articles on modern theologians. The work on this series was an important factor in my decision to write a book on the subject, and many passages of this book originally appeared in those articles.

In the fall of 1953 I had the opportunity of giving large sections of this material before the Adult Forum of the Swarthmore Friends Meeting. This alert and intelligent audience gave me valuable aid by pointing out where I was vague or had failed to make my point.

I should like to extend my thanks to the Board of Managers of Swarthmore College for the leave of absence which made the writing of this book possible.

Last, but not least, I must express gratitude to my students. Five years at Swarthmore College have taught me much about presenting theological issues to an interested but critical laity.

W. H.

Contents

Introduction

This book arises from my conviction that there is a need for the Protestant laity to do more creative thinking about theology. But where is the layman to start? If he picks up a theological book he is likely to find himself baffled by terms that he cannot understand. Theology is as inaccessible to him as one of Einstein's treatises on relativity. Like every other science, theology has its technical terminology, its jargon. What this book tries to do is to introduce the layman to this field of thought in terms that he can understand. We shall use many technical terms, but when we do we shall try to define them.

First, we had better say why theology is necessary. This is by no means immediately apparent even to the devoted layman. J. P. Williams quotes a minister as saying: "I love flowers, but I hate botany; I love religion, but I hate theology." This attitude is widespread and is often based upon good reasons. Theology can become dull or even unchristian. But the answer to poor theology must be good theology, not no theology. We can see why this is so if we analyze what theology is.

"Theology" comes from two Greek words: *Theos*, meaning God, and *logos*, meaning word or rational thought. Therefore theology is a word or rational thought about God. The word

"God" cannot be defined exactly, but it is normally used to represent whatever is believed to be the Ultimate, the Source of everything else, the highest of values, the Source of all other values. God is that which is deemed worthy of being the goal and purpose of life. In light of this, it is almost self-evident that no man can live without theology.

Frequently someone says: "Why bother with theology? The theologians waste their time debating unimportant issues." Let us examine this statement. Why are these issues deemed unimportant? Obviously, the objector has in mind some concept of highest value by which he judges the arguments of theologians valueless. He has a theological position, a belief about the nature of God, which leads him to judge as unimportant the arguments of theologians. In short, even this attack upon theology is a theological attack.

Often we hear people say that it is not what a man believes, it is what he does that is important. This is a half-truth, but like all half-truths it is dangerous. It is half true because, from the Christian viewpoint, theological thinking is not an end in itself. Christianity is to be lived; it is to issue in action; as long as it remains merely thought it is unchristian and futile. But it is a *half*-truth because whatever a man does depends upon what he thinks and what he holds of ultimate value. When the so-called practical man is faced with the problem of deciding how to act in a given situation, he must have some implicit idea of what ends he wishes to obtain, what values ought to be gained from the solution. Furthermore, he must have some concept of the best means of achieving those values. All of this is theology, whether it be implicit or explicit.

The cliché "It's not what a man thinks but what he does

that counts" seemed plausible as long as the great majority of men in our culture had a Christian scale of values. But we live in a world where precisely that scale of values is threatened and questioned. The moral ideals that seemed self-evident truths to our fathers have become problems for our day. Both Communists and Nazis have recognized that there is no simple distinction between what a man believes and what he does. As a result, they put great emphasis upon propaganda, the concerted attempt to change what men think. They knew that if they could change the thoughts of men about the ultimate nature of things and ultimate values, they could change the actions of men. Christian theology is nothing more nor less than the attempt to change the thinking of men so that they will act as Christians.

Because we live in a time when the ultimate meaning of life is questioned, we can no longer dodge such questions. A few years ago men thought that they could ignore ultimate questions and get along with the job of making this world a better place. Education, science, and technology could, they believed, solve all of our problems. But, as Dr. N. M. Pusey, president of Harvard University, pointed out in his already famous address to the Harvard Divinity School, you do not get rid of these ultimate questions by pretending that they are not there. If you ignore them, they rise in perverted and distorted forms to mock you. Dr. Pusey's point is illustrated by totalitarianism, which arises when men can see nothing more ultimate than their state or economic class.

The attempt to think about God leads immediately to a host of related questions which are included under the term "theology." First, there is the question of man's relation to God, the Ultimate Source of things, including what he deems to be good. Thus we must ask about revelation; that is, How does man know what God is like? Can God be discovered by the same methods that discover scientific truth, or must God himself give some revelation of his nature to man? If God must reveal himself, where and how is he revealed?

This leads to the concept of sin. Sin occurs when man is out of harmony with the Source of his being and when he betrays his highest values. It is interesting to notice that even an ostensibly atheist system, like that of Communism, cannot escape the problem of sin. Those who betray what the Communist believes to be the highest values are not called "sinners"; but they are called "Trotskyists," "Wall Street minions," "warmongers," "capitalist imperialists," and so on.

The question of sin leads to the question of salvation. Salvation occurs when a man, in some sense, overcomes the separation between himself and the Source of his being and when he becomes loyal to the highest values. How does man achieve salvation? How does he overcome sin? Why does man sin in the first place? Why does man fail to achieve the highest values? Does he fall into sin naturally? Can he overcome sin and remain true to the highest that he knows by trying hard, or does he need help from beyond himself? Even the man who says that it is not what you believe but what you do that counts must have some answer, implicit or explicit, to these questions before he can act in any situation.

Behind these lie still more questions. How can men best organize themselves to work together for good? That is, what about the Church? Where is everything leading us? Where are we going? For what can we hope? Is this life, the history of man on this planet, the sum total of our opportunity to know the Highest, or is there a life and realm beyond this world in which our values will continue to their fulfillment? Such questions deal with what theologians call "eschatology."

So viewed, there is no escaping theological questions. We simply do not have the alternative of theology or no theology. Our alternatives are either to have a well thought-out theology, a theology which has passed the test of critical thought, or to have a hodgepodge theology of unexamined concepts, prejudices, and feelings. One of the weaknesses of Protestantism today is that so few Protestants know what they believe or why. This is a mistake that is seldom made by the Communist. The Communist party does a very thorough job of training its devotees. No halfhearted, half thought-out religion can stand before the militant discipline of Communism. But we must not suppose that theology is made necessary by the threat of Communism. The Communist threat simply illustrates a basic fact about life.

The events of the twentieth century have led to a rebirth of Protestant theology. Men are once again wrestling with the ultimate questions of life and are trying to find the Christian answers. I hope that this book will help the layman to discover what is going on in theology. This book is not a complete picture; it is an introduction. It ought to lead the reader to further reading and certainly to further thought. The reader may or may not accept one of the theological positions to be described; but the book will have fulfilled its purpose if it helps the reader to work out his own theological position against the background of modern thought.

There are many ways in which one might introduce the layman to modern theology. One of the most obvious would be to discuss certain topics, such as sin, God, salvation, and give various interpretations of each. I believe that such a method would confuse rather than illuminate. Theology has to hang together; it develops into systems of thought in which the answer given to one question throws light upon the next. I have chosen, therefore, to present modern theology by examining various schools of thought. By this means we can illustrate the way in which each of the various systems forms an organic whole.

While this method is, I believe, the most desirable, it has certain shortcomings, and we must emphasize them. In the first place, as someone has said, "All labels are libels." There is always some injustice involved in putting a man into a school of thought. It too quickly identifies him with certain points of view which he may, in fact, repudiate. There is usually some individuality or originality about every thinker that is lost when you treat him as a member of a school of thought. We have tried to bring out individual differences as far as possible, but the reader must realize that this is a weakness of our method that cannot be completely overcome. In a book that intends to be an introduction only, that is a price that perhaps has to be paid.

A second difficulty is that we are continually tempted to overemphasize the differences in viewpoint and to obscure the areas of agreement. We make a school's position clear by distinguishing it from another school. Furthermore, to list all the points of agreement would lead to wearisome repetition. Again, the reader must recall this limitation.

A third difficulty is that if we present theology in terms of modern schools of thought, we find that there are certain important thinkers who are mentioned only in passing and others who are ignored. The question of which theologians should be used to represent a school of thought is, of course, a matter of individual judgment. I cannot expect that everyone will agree with my particular choices.

Although our purpose is to introduce the reader to modern developments in theology, we have to begin with history. The problems which confront us today did not leap suddenly into life during the twentieth century. They were generated by our past and cannot be understood apart from it. We do not have the space to treat the history of Western thought adequately, but we have devoted two chapters to a quick summary of some of the most important elements of its background.

CHAPTER 1

The Growth of Orthodoxy

It is almost impossible to use the term "orthodoxy" without stirring emotions. There are people who hate the thought of being unorthodox. For them orthodoxy, whether in politics, religion, or table manners, is the first necessity of life. To others, it is the most deplorable state into which a man can fall. It is equivalent to being stale, unoriginal, or just plain dull. On the whole, America has been proud of its unorthodoxy, and Americans often have made a new orthodoxy of being unorthodox. I hope that we can leave behind all emotional content of the word in what follows. By orthodox Christianity, I mean something purely descriptive. Orthodox Christianity is that form of Christianity which won the support of the overwhelming majority of Christians and which is expressed by most of the official proclamations or creeds of Christian groups.

At this point someone might object that it would be better to speak of orthodoxies instead of orthodoxy. Does not each of the multiple divisions of Christendom have its own orthodoxy? Each does, but there has been a central core of Christian doctrine that has held the allegiance of most Christians despite their differences. We are interested in that body of agreement.

Our search for orthodoxy must begin with the New Testament. The first Christians did not have any orthodoxy in the sense of a neatly formulated system of thought. Modern critical scholarship of the Bible has found that there are many theologies within the New Testament, but it has also found that beneath these variations in theology there is a common faith. The various theologies are the attempts of earnest men to think out and to express to others this common faith. Much of this faith is implicit rather than explicit. Twenty centuries have not been enough to work out all of the implications that lie in the basic faith of the New Testament.

The New Testament faith is based squarely upon the belief that in the life, death, and resurrection of the man Jesus, God entered into the life of man in a decisive fashion. That is why four accounts of the life of Jesus were passed down to us. That is why Christians faced the threat of dungeon, fire, and sword to spread their "Good News," which is what the word "Gospel" means. It is a distortion of history to suppose that Christianity began because a few men were persuaded by the brilliant ethical teaching of Jesus. On the contrary, the early Christians went out to tell the world of one whom God had proclaimed to be Lord.

We cannot overemphasize the importance of the Resurrection for the early Christians. Paul says, "If Christ be not raised, your faith is vain" (I Cor. 15:17). If you read this passage, you will see that he is not trying to persuade his fellow Christians that Christ arose; rather he is referring to the one point where there can be no difference between himself and his readers in order that he may go on to prove another point. The Resurrection was the one thing the early

Christian could not deny and still consider himself a Christian. It was the rock of his faith.

Today the Resurrection often means to Christians nothing more than proof of life after death. It meant that to the early Christians, but it meant much more. Primarily, the Resurrection was the proof that Jesus was the Christ or Messiah of God. For centuries the Jews had lived on the promise that God was going to send his Messiah, his chosen agent, to save his people and to establish a society of justice. Quite naturally, since the Jews lived for centuries under foreign conquerors, they came to hope that the Messiah would be a military leader who would call upon the legions of heaven to overthrow the cruel oppressors. Finally, when Jesus came his followers dared to hope that he was the long-awaited Messiah. But he did not act as many had hoped the Messiah would act: he did not gather an army; he refused to be made a king. Finally, he was captured and spit upon and led out like a common criminal to be executed. He died beautifully, but the disciples wanted more than a beautiful death. A Messiah who had died, who was defeated and overcome by Rome, was hardly one who could save man. The disciples fled, not because they lacked courage but because there seemed no sense in risking one's life in a lost cause. They had made a tragic mistake and they felt they might as well admit it. But at the very depth of despair they were suddenly faced with a new development. Jesus was not dead: he was alive; he had risen.

What the Resurrection meant, therefore, was that Jesus was after all the Messiah or agent of God. God had been working through him as the disciples had believed. Rome with its naked power was not the most powerful force in the world; Rome had set in motion a train of events that would eventually overcome it when it crucified the lowly Galilean carpenter. The forces of evil—and the early Christians believed that these included the demons as well as evil men—had risen to their greatest power and had done their worst. But, in the very moment of their victory, God had proved himself more powerful than they. Jesus had not achieved what they had hoped he would achieve, but as the days passed they realized that he had achieved something better. He had not freed them from Rome, but he had freed them from the chains that bound them to sin and death, chains that had held them in fear. He had revealed decisively that the power of good is greater than the power of evil.

In the Resurrection God had proved the superiority of the spirit of Jesus over the spirit of evil. Therefore the Christians looked forward to the return or Second Coming of Christ, when evil would be completely destroyed. The forces of evil had been defeated in the crucial battle; there could be no further doubt about the ultimate victor. But the evil forces were still in the field and still able to cause discomfort. The decisive battle had been won but the final battle was still to come.

The disciples went out into the pagan world with the message that God had spoken, God had acted, God had revealed his nature to man. Man need no longer climb the treacherous mountain path that leads to knowledge of God; God had come down from the mountain to allow men to see him. "God," they proclaimed, "was in Christ, reconciling the world unto himself" (2 Cor. 5:19).

Though this faith was simple, it was full of implications. It meant that God was like Jesus; the spirit of Jesus revealed the nature of God. In a world where many voices were raised claiming to know all about God, the Christians dared to believe that God himself had broken through the clouds which hid his face. The one word that described the life and teaching of Jesus was "love." If God was like Jesus, then "God is love" (I John 4:8).

As time passed, the early term "Messiah," or "Christ," as it was translated into Greek, no longer seemed adequate to express this faith. This was particularly true as Christians went out to the Greek and Roman world where people had never heard of the Jewish Messiah. And so they began to call Jesus the "Lord," "Savior," "only begotten Son." All of these were terms by which Christians tried to express their belief that in Jesus God had made a unique revelation of himself to man. Finally, they came to say with Doubting Thomas, "My Lord and my God." Jesus had not been simply sent by God; he was God, God at work in the life of man.

Paul, the leading interpreter of Christianity during the New Testament period, led Christianity in its earliest battle —that against legalism. Every religion, including the Christian, tends to become legalistic. That is, it teaches that man must obey certain rules and regulations to win the favor and rewards of God.

Both Jesus and Paul fought against legalism. Jesus asserted that when a man had done everything that he could, he still was to count himself an unprofitable servant (Luke 17:10). That is, he was not to suppose that he had earned some kind of payment from God. Similarly, Jesus taught that

God makes his rain to fall on the just and on the unjust (Matt. 5:45). God does not place an umbrella over the heads of those who are good so that they have a special protection from the slings and arrows of outrageous fortune. The slowness with which Christians have come to accept this basic fact in Jesus' teaching is strange. It still seems natural for many to suppose that a life of superior goodness will receive a superior reward, if not here, then surely hereafter. Jesus, however, explicitly denies this in his parable of the Laborers in the Vineyard (Matt. 20:1-16). The men who have worked from the dew of early morn and through the noontide heat do not receive any more pay at the end of the day than the men who worked but an hour.

The early Christians, led by Paul, came to see that legalism, the attempt to earn rewards from God by obeying certain rules, is basically wrong. It is wrong because it commercializes religion. One is good because he expects to get paid for his good deeds. It is wrong because it leads so easily to pride and hypocrisy, as we see in the Pharisees. Because the Pharisee keeps the law a little better than others, he feels far superior. Furthermore, he is continually tempted into the hypocrisy of believing that he is doing better than he really is. On the other hand, men like Paul found that legalism led to despair. As they realized how far short they were falling of the ideal goodness, they despaired of themselves, their salvation, and their reward.

In place of legalism, Jesus and Paul put the doctrine of salvation by grace through faith. The doctrine is implicit in Jesus and explicit in Paul. It is rooted in Jesus' assertion that God is a father. Every child who has loving parents knows the meaning of salvation by grace. The child does not earn his way into his parents' favor; he is loved simply because he exists. Before the child knows the meaning of love, he is surrounded with the tangible proofs of his parents' love. The true parent does not shower greater gifts upon the good son than upon the less good. True family life is not built upon a commercial basis of so much love for so much work; it is built freely upon grace, unearned love. The child is motivated, not by the desire to win greater favors from his parents, but by gratitude for the favors he has already received.

When the child from such a home "goes wrong," when he disappoints the hopes of his parents, he does not have to earn his way back into their favor. The parable of the Prodigal Son is a beautiful presentation of salvation by grace. After the son had disgraced his home and besmirched his own and his family's good name by riotous living with harlots, he found himself hobnobbing with the pigs. As he eked out his living with husks, he decided upon a scheme to earn his way back into his father's good graces. He would become a servant in his father's home. He had a nice little speech prepared, in which he was to offer himself as a servant to his father. But his father never gave him a chance to speak it. While the son was yet far off, the father ran to him and accepted him as a son, not as a servant.

We must be careful not to interpret this too sentimentally. It is not simply a matter of letting bygones be bygones. The true parent does not simply condone the erring boy. Robert Louis Stevenson, in *The Master of Ballantrae*, has told the story of a father who did simply condone his son's sin. Stevenson says of the father that forgiveness—to misuse a noble word—flowed from him like the weak tears of senility. True parental forgiveness is not like the tears of senility; it is rather like the Cross on Golgotha; it hurts the parent; it rends his soul. It is not easy to embrace the neck that was last caressed by harlots; it is not easy to forget the scorn and ridicule of the neighbors; but, despite the cost, the father forgives.

It is this family relationship which Jesus and Paul use to illustrate the free grace of God. God's love is not something that man has to purchase or deserve. "While we were yet sinners," says Paul, "Christ died for us" (Rom. 5:8). That is, before man had made himself good enough, God acted to save him. Through Jesus, God offers to man the promise that if he will but turn to God he will be received. This forgiveness is not an easy matter for God. Although Paul does not have any clear doctrine of the meaning of the Cross, he is certain that it represents the price that God had to pay to win man from sin. This forgiveness of God could be received by any man who would accept it in faith.

Faith does not mean, for Paul, believing something, although of course some belief must be involved in it. Faith is rather a giving of oneself. The Prodigal Son had faith when he arose to go home. Faith is, for Paul, a commitment which causes one to act in a certain fashion. Faith in God did not mean believing that there was a God or believing some doctrine about Jesus; it meant giving oneself over to being a son of God, to having that mind in oneself which was in Christ Jesus (Phil. 2:5).

It would be a mistake, however, to suppose that grace was

simply God's willingness to forgive the man who came to him with faith. Grace also included the power of God which comes to a man and enables him to do those things that he could not do before. Jesus asserts that faith can move mountains, and Paul concedes that through faith he has found the power that he lacked to do those things which he had known that he ought to do but which he had not done. Paul teaches that we can live "in Christ" a new life of strength and power.

The grace of God frees a man from fear and the sense of guilt. He knows that he is accepted, even as he is, by God. He knows that neither life nor death nor principalities nor powers can remove him from the love of God that is in Christ Jesus (Rom. 8:38-39). But it also frees him from the bonds of habit, indolence, and weakness that tie him to sin. Down through Christian history men have affirmed that in Christ they found two great freedoms: the freedom from fear and the freedom from sin.

This was the simple core of Christian faith upon which Christian orthodoxy was built. Orthodoxy grew from the life that was lived in the light of this basic faith. Christian theology is not a philosophical system that was thought up by men in the quiet of an academic study. It was hammered out by men who were on the firing line of the Church. Every plank in the platform of orthodoxy was laid because some heresy had arisen which threatened to change the nature of Christianity and to destroy its central faith. In facing heresy, Christians were forced to think out the implications of their convictions. Because the doctrines of Christianity grew out of life and not out of classroom discussion, they cannot be understood by the man who, figuratively speaking, puts his feet on the mantelpiece and reads about them. They can only be understood by the man who shares the Christian life, who is ready to stand, as the writers of the doctrines stood, in the front lines of Christian living.

Like "orthodoxy," "heresy" is an emotionally charged term. We mean by it a misinterpretation of the orthodox position. The first great heresy, Gnosticism, arose in the second and third centuries. It was a movement that threatened Christianity from within at a time when the Roman emperors were threatening it from without, and of the two threats the Gnostics were the more dangerous. Rome could not kill Christianity, but Gnosticism, if it had been successful, would have perverted it.

The Gnostics were philosophers who wished to amalgamate all the world's religions by taking the best in each of them. In due time, many Gnostics found their way into the Church. They began to link up their ideas with Christianity, but in doing so they changed Christianity to fit their ideas.

The basic belief of the Gnostics was what we call dualism. That is, they believed that the world is ultimately divided between two powers, good and evil. In line with much Greek philosophy, they identified evil with matter. Because of this they rejected the God of the Old Testament who had created the world. The Creator of this evil world must be evil, they insisted.

Because the Gnostics identified evil with the material world, they sought salvation from it. All material things were evil and hindered the salvation of the soul. They believed that the soul could save itself by an ascetic denial of the flesh and by knowledge. In fact, the name Gnostic comes from the Greek word *gnosis*, which means knowledge. They were particularly concerned with the mystical forms of knowledge. Knowledge was to be kept secret and revealed only to the elite few who were initiated into the mysteries and who were worthy of learning the truth.

The Gnostics liked many things about Christianity. They liked the concept of Christ being sent by God. They taught that the good God had sent one of his subordinates, Christ, into the world to free the souls of men from the chains of matter into which they had been locked by the evil God of the Old Testament. Christ, however, could not allow his purity to be tainted by matter. He could not have been truly a man. It was not right that Christ should have been born of woman because, even if the woman was a virgin, they felt he could not have escaped contamination. It was equally unthinkable that the divine Christ should have eaten and drunk, have grown weary, and suffered and died. Different Gnostics used different arguments to get out of this dilemma. One group insisted that the divine Christ had adopted the human Jesus for a short time and had acted and spoken through him, but had fled from Jesus before the crucifixion. Another group insisted that Jesus did not really have a body at all; it was a clever hallucination. Whichever school a Gnostic belonged to, he agreed in denying that Jesus was in any sense a true human being. This Christian heresy did not deny that Jesus was divine; it denied that Jesus was human.

The Gnostics were very difficult to combat, for most of

them lived pure lives. In a day when asceticism was widely extolled, their rigorous denial of the flesh won them considerable favor. In arguments they would always insist that they had some secret information that had been denied their opponent: Jesus had passed on this information to the elite Gnostics of his time and had hidden it from the materially blinded Jews who founded the Church. If this failed, Gnostics would claim a special revelation from heaven which proved their point. Yet Christianity had to cast out Gnosticism. If the Gnostics had triumphed, the message of Christianity to all men would have been replaced by a message for the chosen few. Its Christ would have ceased to be a human being and would have become like one of the many gods of the mystery religions—a vague and legendary figure. Christians would have been forced to abandon their priceless heritage from Judaism and become a world-denying ascetic band.

Christianity rose up to cast out this heresy, and in doing so it solidified its own orthodox position. The Apostles' Creed, which is still repeated in many churches, arose at this time, and can best be understood as a refutation of Gnosticism. First, it affirmed belief in "God, the Father Almighty, Maker of heaven and earth." That is, it repudiated the idea that the created world is evil or the work of an evil god. This material world is good and worthy to be used and enjoyed by man.

The Apostles' Creed next affirms belief in "Jesus Christ His only Son our Lord: who was conceived by the Holy Ghost, born of the Virgin Mary, suffered under Pontius Pilate, was crucified, dead and buried." Many a modern man has been stopped by the phrase "born of the Virgin Mary."

He cannot believe in the Virgin Birth. But, ironically, to the early Gnostic, the problem was not "Virgin"; it was "born." The modern man sees a red flag because he hears "born of the *Virgin* Mary"; the Gnostic saw a red flag because he heard "*born* of the Virgin Mary." Actually, this phrase, together with the ones about suffering, death, and burial, was the Church's method of asserting its belief in the complete humanity of Jesus. Whatever orthodox Christianity had to say about the divinity of Jesus, it retained a firm hold on its belief in his humanity.

In the same light must be understood that other phrase of the Creed that causes trouble to many moderns—"The Resurrection of the body." Are we to believe, they ask, that the atoms of this earthly body will be regathered and made to live again? Actually, anyone who has read the fifteenth chapter of First Corinthians could not suppose that this is what the doctrine means. But it was a method of asserting the Jewish faith that man is a whole; he is not divided, as the Gnostics and many other Greek philosophers believed, into a good soul and an evil body. The Gnostic doctrine of the immortality of the soul is based on this belief, and implies that the soul is naturally immortal and only needs to be freed from the flesh. This also implies that the body is at best a burden and at worst an obstacle to the salvation of the soul. Christianity denied this, asserting the value of the body and thereby the importance of this earthly life.

The next great issue that came to the center of Christian thinking was that of the Trinity—the relationship of Father, Son, and Holy Spirit. This too was raised by the problem of heresy. Christians never sat down to think out the doctrine of the Trinity as a philosophical problem. Augustine summed it up when he said that the pronouncements upon the subject were not made to say something but in order that Christians might not be silent. That is, concepts had arisen which made silence impossible.

After considerable reflection, I have decided that it is impossible for me to make this doctrine clear to the reader in the space that I can devote to it. The best minds in Christendom debated for centuries before they came to any conclusion, and that debate, presupposing a full knowledge of the philosophies of the time, cannot be explained briefly. I shall limit myself to a few observations that will be helpful for our purpose.

The problem was debated at the Council of Nicea in 325, from which we get the Nicene Creed found in the hymnbooks or Prayer Books of many modern denominations. Most people have heard the gibe that the Council of Nicea saw a battle that nearly split Christendom apart and that the battle was over nothing but one "iota," the smallest letter in the Greek alphabet. It is true that the two sides at Nicea were fighting over which of two words should be put into the creed and that the only difference in the spelling of the words was one Greek letter. One side wanted the word "homoousios" to say that Christ was of the same substance as God, and the other side wanted the word "homoiousios" to say that Christ was of a substance like to that of God. But only ignorance can go from that fact to the conclusion that the issues must have been unimportant.

I recall a story which appeared in a popular magazine a few years ago. It explained why telegraph and cable companies spell out punctuation marks instead of having just one signal for each of them. At one time, according to the story, there was a code signal for each punctuation mark. A woman, touring in Europe, cabled her husband as follows: "Have found wonderful bracelet. Price seventy-five thousand dollars. May I buy it?" The husband promptly cabled back, "No, price too high." The cable operator, in transmitting the message, missed the signal for the comma. The woman received a message which read, "No price too high." She bought the bracelet; the husband sued the company and won. Ever since, the users of Morse code have spelled out punctuation. This anecdote serves to remind us that the importance of a message cannot be weighed by the size of the punctuation or the number of letters involved. Although only an iota divided the parties at Nicea, the issues involved represented two completely different interpretations of the Christian faith.

The problem of the Trinity arises from the Christian belief that God was acting in and through Jesus Christ. In the fourth century Arius put forward the theory that Christ was a lesser god created by God. This lesser god came to earth in the man Jesus who was not really a man at all, but a divine being freed from the normal limitations of humanity. If the Arian party could have got their iota into the creed, their point of view would have become orthodox Christianity. It would have meant that Christianity had degenerated to the polytheistic stage of paganism. It would have had two gods and a Jesus who was neither God nor man. It would have meant that God himself was unapproachable and apart from man. The result would have been to make of Christianity another pagan mystery religion.

The Nicene Creed asserted that God and Christ were of the same substance. This was the attempt to say in the philosophy of the time that there is only one God. He is active in creating and sustaining the world (as the Father); he was in Jesus Christ (as the Son); and he moves in the heart of the believer (as the Holy Spirit). The Nicene Creed rejected any attempt to think of three gods bound into some kind of unity. Christians have often come to think of Father, Son, and Holy Spirit as three gods, but when they have done so, they have erred from the path of orthodoxy. The criticism, made by Mohammedans, Jews, and Unitarians, that orthodox Christianity has three gods and that it has lost the monotheism of the Old Testament is based upon misunderstanding.

One of the complicating factors is that Trinitarian doctrine speaks of "Three Persons" but one God. The word "person" did not mean to the early thinkers what it means today. To us, a person means someone like Tom, Dick, or Harry. But the Latin word *persona* originally meant a mask which was worn by an actor on the stage. In Trinitarian thought the "mask" is not worn by God to hide but to reveal his true character. It is clear that when we think of the Trinity, we should not try to think of three persons in our sense of the term. Augustine's interpretation became orthodox, if not universal, for the West. He believed that if man is created in the image of God, he is created in the image of the Trinity. Hence he used analogies from the human mind to explain the Trinity. The Trinity is like the memory, intelligence, and will in the mind of a man. In short, as Augustine interprets the Trinity, we do not have to think of three persons when we think of God; but we may think of one person. Of course, Augustine made it clear that this was only an analogy; he was far too profound a thinker to suppose that God was a glorified man sitting in heaven. But if we are to speak at all about the mystery that is God, we must speak in analogies, and the analogy for the Trinity is not three men but one.

The Trinity was important, not simply because it saved Christianity from the return to paganism but because it also gave the Christian assurance that it was God who was in, and responsible for, Jesus Christ. Man's salvation did not hang from the slender thread of what man himself had achieved, nor did it depend upon what some divine being less than God had done. Man could have the courage to overcome fear and doubt because God himself had acted for him and had revealed himself as a God of love and mercy.

The Trinitarian controversy was followed by what we know as the Christological controversy. This controversy was fought out in the Council of Chalcedon in 451 and issued in the Creed of Chalcedon. In a sense, it may be said that the Trinitarian controversy was over the nature of God in heaven. What is God like, if Jesus was divine? The Christological doctrine tried to see what Jesus, on earth, was like if he were divine. Nicea had decided that there was but one God and that Jesus was fully divine, the act of the one God. But immediately men began to wonder how Jesus could be both divine and human. How could the eternal, unchanging, perfect God take on the limitations of a man? Many people felt that he could not.

One group of thinkers, known as Apollinarians, arose who,

in effect, admitted that Jesus had a human body (they could not deny that without falling into the old Gnostic error), but they denied that he had a true human personality. The Second Person of the Trinity took the place of a human personality in Jesus' body. Despite the fact that Jesus was allowed a body, this did not make him any more human than the Gnostics had done. It was still impossible to believe with the Bible that he "was in all points tempted like as we are" (Heb. 4:15). The other side argued that there were two natures in Jesus, a human spirit and the spirit of God. These two became fused by the fact that the human Jesus gave himself over completely to the divine so that there was a moral unity. This view, known as Nestorianism, gave Jesus moral freedom and the possibility of temptation, but it seemed to leave Jesus with a dual or even with a split personality.

The decision at Chalcedon is altogether too complex to analyze in our space, and authorities still debate its implications. But this fact can be seen: the orthodox faith was settled as the belief that Jesus was truly divine, the work of God, and that he was truly and completely human. Chalcedon repudiated any theory that would deny either the humanity or the divinity of Jesus. There is no doubt that this was the faith of the earliest Christians, and as such Chalcedon was true to that faith. But it is also clear that the problem of how Christ could be both human and divine remains unsolved. We shall see that the question arises again in modern theology.

It is easy to be critical of those early Church conferences at Nicea and Chalcedon. There were many instances of petty personal jealousies, national clashes, political maneuvering, and power politics. And yet, as one looks back over the perspective of history, it is hard to doubt that some divine guidance was also at work. Despite the mortal weaknesses that were so evident, the Church set its face squarely against the forces which would have robbed Christianity of its monotheism and its historical Jesus and which would have pulled Christianity down to the level of pagan faiths. It is well to keep this in mind as we grow impatient with very similar mortal weaknesses that are evident in the present World Council of Churches as it tries to think through the implications of faith for today. It is easy for us to see its weakness, but future historians may also see the hand of God in the work of the Council.

The great father of orthodoxy for Western thought was Augustine. He is a Catholic saint, and yet the Protestant Reformation leaned more heavily upon him than upon any other pre-Reformation thinker. We have already mentioned his contribution to the doctrine of the Trinity. Augustine was one of those rare mental geniuses who occur once in a thousand years. Modern thought owes him many an unacknowledged debt. Augustine drove men's thoughts inward to self-analysis, and, as one modern writer has pointed out, about the only thing Augustine could learn from modern psychology would be its jargon. Unfortunately, we can mention only one aspect of this great thinker's contribution: it was he who brought most forcefully into orthodox thought the concept of Original Sin.

Before Augustine, Christian thought had expressed its faith that Jesus, as the revelation of God, was also the revelation of what man was created to be. But, if this is the case, something seems to have gone wrong. Man, with his pettiness, his vindictiveness, his ceaseless crimes, both those of commission and of omission, is far from having in him the spirit that was in Jesus. To this, orthodoxy had said that man had fallen. Adam, the first man, had used his God-given freedom of choice to choose against God and had pulled mankind down with him. Christ was sent to restore man to his original position.

Augustine's doctrine, like the rest of orthodoxy, was worked out against a heresy. The heresy was that of an English monk, Pelagius. Pelagius insisted that every man is completely free to choose either good or evil at every moment in his life. He insisted that Adam's fall had affected no one but Adam. Against this Augustine denied that man is free in this sense to do either good or evil. Working with what reminds us of modern depth psychology, Augustine insisted that the pull of the race is stronger than Pelagius realized. The individual cannot start with a clean slate; he bears his society, his heritage, with him. Because that heritage is sinful, man is prone to sin; he has a bias toward sin so great that, but for the helping grace of God, he cannot overcome it. Instead of being free, man is actually bound to his way of sin and only becomes truly free as God gives him the grace to break through his bonds.

Augustine located the source of original sin, that is, the inherited weakness or inability to do good, in man's pride. Turning to the story of Adam, Augustine pointed out that Adam was free; he had everything he could desire in the Garden of Eden. But Adam desired one more thing: he desired to be free from God; he resented his dependence upon God; he wished to take the place of God. So, at the lure of the serpent that he might become as God, he ate the fruit of the tree. That is, man's refusal to accept his position as a creature, to be what he was made, leads him to seek to be equal with God, his creator. When man refuses to give God the proper place in life, the result is concupiscence, the unrestrained lust after the things of this world. Because God ceases to be the center of life, man falls into the other sins: greed, lust, robbery, murder, selfishness. The word "concupiscence," however, had also the implications of sex. At first, with Augustine, sex was only one of the many lusts for the things of the world which plague man; but there was a tendency both in Augustine and in his followers to emphasize sex above the other sins.

Adam's sin was passed down to his descendants. Because each descendant is procreated through sex, there is a twofold source of sin. The sexual origin of each man is sinful, and the tendency to sin is also inherited as a congenital weakness.

If we are to understand the modern theologians who return to this doctrine, we must see that in Augustine there are actually two distinct elements. First, there is a psychological analysis of man. According to this, pride, which is a basic weakness of man, explains the great gulf between what man was created to be and what he is. Here the source of man's ills is a spiritual one. But, in explaining how this began and how it is transmitted, you have Augustine's doctrine about Adam and the inheritance of his sinful traits. It would almost seem that the spiritual nature of sin has been turned into a biological taint. It is not easy to reconcile the spiritual analysis of sin with the biological transmission of it. Certainly, it is possible, as we shall see, to agree with Augustine's spiritual analysis while rejecting his theory of inheritance.

Augustine's theory led him to the doctrine of predestination. This never became orthodox for all Christians, but we meet it again in Calvinistic orthodoxy. If man cannot save himself, if God's grace must save him, how does God decide whom he will aid? It cannot be, felt Augustine, that God foresees someone earning grace, for it is a free gift. If you read Augustine's *Confessions*, the autobiography of his spiritual life, you will find him expressing again and again his wonder that God had saved *him*. He was certain that he had done nothing to deserve it. It was no credit to him that he no longer walked the paths of error and sin in which once he had delighted. God had acted upon him in a way that could not have been foreseen. God had chosen or elected him for salvation.

When the Reformation occurred, the Reformers did not, for the most part, question any of these doctrines of orthodoxy that we have been tracing. Luther returned to the doctrine of salvation by grace, emphasizing it in a way in which it had not been emphasized since Paul. This brought him into sharp conflict with the Catholic doctrines about the nature of the Church and authority within it. Renouncing the pope's claim to supremacy, Luther found the ultimate authority in the Bible as it was interpreted by the Holy Spirit working within a man's heart. In the place of the Catholic hierarchy he placed the doctrine of the priesthood of all believers. That is, no man needed a priest to mediate between him and God except Christ, who is the perfect mediator, the perfect priest for all men.

Calvin followed Luther and gave us the first systematic Protestant theology. The center of theology for Calvin was God and his chief aim was to glorify God. Any kind of faith in the natural ability or power of man was, to Calvin, faith in a bruised and broken reed. But where man was helpless, God was almighty. God could be trusted to do what man could not. Thus Calvin followed Augustine's doctrine of predestination.

The doctrine of predestination is difficult for modern man to understand. Yet, ironically, modern man is quite ready to accept theories of determinism which deny any freedom or dignity to man. These modern doctrines are more hopeless than those of Calvin, for there is no God of mercy in them to modify the iron necessity of determinism. Predestination was important for the Calvinist as a basis for assurance. The Roman Catholic was certain of his salvation because he was in the one true Church. The Protestants took the courageous step of repudiating such certainty and risked their salvation itself in order that they might follow their consciences. The doctrine of predestination was the Calvinist answer to Catholic certainty. The salvation of man does not depend, said Calvin, upon membership in an institution. Salvation is a matter between a man and his God. We must trust God to save his elect. The differences that divide one group of men from another are of no importance to God.

There is one last plank in the platform of orthodoxy that must be mentioned, the doctrine of atonement. Every religion has had to deal with the concept of atonement. If you believe that God has any requirements which man fails to fulfill, then you are faced with the problem of how God can be reconciled. If you have injured a friend or neighbor, you have the problem of atonement, the problem of reestablishing the fellowship that has been broken.

In contrast to other religions, Christianity has a unique point of view. Whereas most religions believe that man has to do something to atone to God, Christianity teaches that God himself has performed the atoning work. Other religions perform sacrifices in order that God might turn his angry face back toward man and forgive him. Christianity teaches that God has performed a sacrifice, in and through Jesus, which has brought God and man back into fellowship with each other. But the problem arises: What did God do? Paul is clear that Jesus' death was central, but he gives no clear explanation. The Church never held a council on this doctrine, as it did on the Trinity and the nature of Christ. No one doctrine has been held from the beginning, and hence it is difficult to speak of the orthodox position.

The so-called classical doctrine of atonement was accepted for more than a thousand years. According to this, Satan had gained the souls of men because they had sinned. But God made a bargain with Satan: he would give Satan the soul of Jesus, even though Satan did not deserve him, if Satan would release the souls of men who accepted Jesus. Satan agreed, thinking that Jesus was only a good man. But when he received Jesus, he found that he could not hold him for he was the Son of God. And so Satan ended up with neither the souls of those who accepted Christ nor Christ himself. This doctrine sounds crude and seems to implicate God in a rather shady trick upon the Devil. It has, none the less, two profound thoughts. It expresses faith that in the death and resurrection of Jesus, God has conquered the forces of evil. Good is more powerful than evil. In the second place, it points to the fact that evil tends to overreach and thus destroy itself. "Give a man enough rope and he will hang himself." This is a fact of life. If Hitler, for example, had been content with a little less he might still rule Germany. Evil cannot be satisfied, and in its insatiable greed it brings destruction upon itself. But despite these insights, the doctrine seemed too crude, and in the eleventh century two new doctrines were put forward.

The first came from Anselm. He argued that man owed obedience to God, the ruler of the universe, but he had failed to obey and hence he fell into debt to God. He had dishonored God. Justice demanded either that the debt be paid to God or that man be punished. Either way would uphold God's prestige as the moral ruler of man. But God did not want to punish man eternally, for his purpose in creating man was to have fellowship with him. Man could not give God satisfaction since man already owed perfect obedience and could do no more. If God waved the sin aside and simply forgave, his honor and prestige as the ruler would be called into question. We have a dilemma; man owed the debt, but only God could pay it. So, God sent Jesus, who was both God and man. Because he was God, he could pay the debt; because he was also man he could pay it for man. But even Jesus could not pay it by living a perfect life, for, as man, he already owed that to God. But Jesus did not deserve to die since he had not sinned. Consequently, when Jesus gave himself over to death, he paid the debt for man. God's honor was vindicated so that he could forgive those who came to him through Christ.

This theory did not express perfectly what the Church wanted to say and it was never accepted officially. It made God sound very much like a feudal lord who was afraid his serfs might get out of hand if he appeared too lenient. Yet it did express the Church's belief that forgiveness is not something simple or easy. It costs God to forgive.

Abélard presented another theory. He insisted that there was nothing on God's side that made forgiveness impossible. But forgiveness is a two-way affair. You cannot forgive a man who does not wish to be forgiven. Forgiveness means the restoration of broken fellowship; but one cannot restore the fellowship if the other does not wish it restored. This, says Abélard, was God's problem. He wanted to forgive man, but man went his merry way sinning and did not repent or ask forgiveness. So God acted; he sent his Son to suffer and die for man as a manifestation of God's great love. When man sees this he is moved to shame and repents so that God is able to forgive him.

Abélard's doctrine also says something that orthodox Christianity wanted to say. In the death of Christ we see the love of God in such a way that we are moved to repent. None the less, Abélard's doctrine won him the charge of heresy. The orthodox argument against it usually goes like this: If a man jumps into the water and saves me while I am drowning, the act reveals his love. But if we are walking along the beach and he suddenly says, "See how much I love you," and then jumps into the water and drowns, we are inclined to think the sun got too hot for him. In other words, Christ's death can only be a revelation of God's love for man if it was a necessary sacrifice. It is meaningless if man could be saved without it.

Orthodox Christianity, while it was not completely satisfied with Anselm, usually has taken some form of his theory. Christ, it has believed, was in some sense our substitute; he died to pay our debt or he suffered the punishment that we ought to have suffered for our sin. Protestant orthodoxy was inclined to put the doctrine in terms of the law courts. Man had committed crimes for which he must be punished, but Jesus "took the rap" in man's place. So interpreted, the doctrine has the effect of Abélard's; it wins man to repent, but it does so because the sacrifice was a necessary one and not a grand gesture.

This is the main outline of the orthodox position in theology upon which Christians from widely separated denominations would agree. It is this body of thought, with a few implications that we shall see as we go along, that we have in mind when we speak of orthodox Christianity.

CHAPTER 2

The Threat to Orthodoxy

In the last chapter we spoke of the rise of orthodoxy. Even there it was evident that not all Christians were orthodox, for orthodoxy was normally clarified only when someone put forth a heresy. In this chapter we will concentrate upon the unorthodox. If we were attempting a complete history of unorthodoxy, we should begin here with the early Christians as we did in the last chapter. But our purpose is not that; we desire only to interpret the modern field and so will limit ourselves to what is helpful for that purpose. Since our concern is with Protestant thought, we will limit ourselves to the period since the Reformation.

As man entered the modern world, there was a twofold threat to orthodoxy. One threat came from outside the Church and spoke through secular philosophies. The other threat came from within the Church itself, where an increasing number of Christians became dissatisfied with orthodoxy. There is a relation between these two movements but there is also a distinction. We shall first look at the secular thought and later return to developments within Christianity itself. Since the secular developments are better known than the religious, we shall deal more fully with the latter.

At the time of the Reformation there was another powerful current of thought, already two hundred years old: the

Renaissance. It began by looking back and rediscovering the ancient Greek and Roman culture in which was to be found a spirit of life quite different from that of medieval Europe. Some of the Renaissance thinkers were indifferent or antagonistic to religion; some were friendly to religion; and some, like Melanchthon and Zwingli, were leaders of the Reformation. But there was a tendency in most of the Renaissance thinkers to leave orthodoxy. Erasmus, for example, tried to be a loyal son of the Roman Catholic Church, but his writings won the condemnation of his Church's authorities.

The Renaissance was characterized by faith in man and interest in this world. Compared to the medieval preoccupation with life after death, the Renaissance was relatively uninterested in the subject. Because of the Renaissance's faith in reason, it did not see any necessity for revelation from God. It was not interested in theology or in the sacramental aspects of the Church. Religion to the thinkers of this school was the cornerstone of ethics.

The Renaissance was deeply interested in restoring the thought of the ancient world and began to work out a science to restore the original wording of manuscripts. In due time, this interest led men to reconsider the manuscripts of the Bible, and here was one place where Erasmus won the displeasure of his Church. Luther, however, in translating the Bible, made use of these results of Renaissance scholarship.

The eighteenth century, the century of rationalism and enlightenment, brought the strongest secular blows against orthodoxy. The rationalists were men who believed in reason with a profound faith. They rebelled against all authorities outside man's reason and claimed for reason an autonomy which would enable it to examine all questions without interference. The rationalists were by no means irreligious men. John Locke, for example, believed that no tolerance could be shown to atheists, for they threatened the very structure of Western civilization upon which tolerance and our other ideals must rest. But if rationalism was not anti-religious, it was anti-orthodox. It wanted a religion, as Kant put it, within the bounds of reason only.

Among the attacks of rationalism upon orthodoxy was Hume's argument against the likelihood of miracles. Hume did not deny the possibility of miracles; his own philosophy would have made such a denial contradictory. But he did argue that miracles would always be less probable than some alternative explanation. Despite the fact that Hume's argument tended to be circular, he was widely hailed as having disproved miracles. It became next to impossible for orthodoxy to prove the truth of its faith by pointing to the miracle stories of the Bible.

Immanuel Kant attacked the so-called "proofs of God." These were not necessarily central to orthodoxy, for the Church did not worry much about proving God until the thirteenth century, when Thomas Aquinas supplied his famous five proofs. Nevertheless, it shook orthodoxy to find that reason could not establish beyond doubt the existence of God. Kant himself argued that if pure reason could not find God, the practical demands of moral living could. But Kant's God was hardly the God of orthodoxy. For Kant only three religious postulates were necessary for the moral life: God, the freedom of man, and immortality.

Although Kant, in his last writings, returned to a concept

of radical evil, the rationalists as a whole were opposed to any doctrine of original sin. They had great confidence that man's reason was good and could solve all of man's problems.

At the same time that rationalism was attacking orthodox religion, natural science was arising. Many foolish things have been written about the conflict of science and religion. Usually science is pictured as a knight in shining armor, always following the gleam of truth, while religion is the stupid dragon that tries to devour truth. This picture, which owes much to Andrew Dickson White's monumental work *A History of the Warfare of Science with Theology in Christendom*, is only partly true. In every conflict over science, there were many sincerely religious and orthodox men who fought for the acceptance of science. On the other hand, there were many men of science who fought against the new scientific developments. We need another book to balance the scales, one which might be called *A History of the Warfare of Science with Science*. Actually, what happened was that the whole cultural feeling of an age rose up in protest against new world views that would shatter the comfortable picture of the universe that was accepted. Religion, as a powerful and organized force in society, often became the center of the anti-scientific protest. As a result, religion, particularly in its orthodox forms, became discredited. It seemed that science was always proved right and religion wrong. The idea began to arise that science could solve all of man's problems, that it was only ignorance and inertia, particularly the ignorance and inertia of the Churches, which were holding back the forward march of science, the new savior.

There were two doctrines of science that particularly disturbed orthodox religion, those of Copernicus and Darwin. The medieval world pictured a universe in which the earth was the center and man the supreme form of life upon earth. Copernicus opened the door to a universe so vast that the earth shrank to a mere grain of sand, lost in space. It seemed ridiculous to many people to suppose that either the earth or man could be important to God, if there was a God. Darwin's theory of evolution broke down the barriers between man and the animal world. Man appeared as simply a highly developed animal. In place of the intelligent love of a Creator who gave each animal its shape and form, Darwin pictured a ruthless struggle for existence among life forms, with victory going to those best fitted to survive.

Although at first the doctrine of evolution seemed to doom man to an unending battle for existence, it came in time to lay a foundation for the high hopes of progress that had grown in the rationalist movement. Herbert Spencer was particularly responsible for this. Man had evolved to his present high estate from the amoeba and he was destined, by a law of nature, to keep on progressing to perfection. The orthodox picture of the fall of man was made to look ridiculous. Man had not fallen; he had started out as a mere beast and, over a relatively short time, considering the age of the universe, had risen to unbelievable heights. Before him stretched an unending future of promise. This idea gripped both the intellectuals and the man in the street. The continual advance of invention led the average man to look condescendingly upon the ways of his fathers and to look forward to the even greater things that were to come. As Harry

Emerson Fosdick said, man no longer desired to die and go to heaven; he wanted to live a hundred years to see what new wonders the inventive genius of man would bring forth.

As man began to look ahead with hope, he became increasingly dissatisfied with the imperfections of his social system. Karl Marx became a leading spokesman for the hope of a better earthly society. As he saw it, religion was one of the barriers to a better earthly life. Religion fed men upon hopes of heaven so that they did not revolt against those who were exploiting them in this life. Even among those who did not follow Marx, there was a widespread feeling that orthodox religion was an enemy of man's hope for a better and more decent life.

With the rise of modern psychology, Freud added new charges against religion. Not only was religion outmoded in its world view, the enemy of science and of progress, it was also, Freud claimed, wish fulfillment, a childish refusal to face the facts of life. By the end of the nineteenth century it had become increasingly impossible for the intellectuals to hold any religion and almost completely impossible for them to hold orthodox Christianity. Nietzsche spoke for a growing number when he proclaimed that "God is dead." Yet there were a few who trembled at the implications. For as Nietzsche saw so clearly, if God is dead, so are the moral traditions of the ages. Man is to replace God by remaking morality, and it is the supermen who must remake it.

If religion in general and orthodoxy in particular were having a difficult time in the secular world, orthodoxy was equally under attack within religion. We must now look at this.

The Reformation was not one movement but four, although the four were vitally related. In addition to the Lutheran and Calvinist movements, there was, in England, the Anglican movement. And, in both England and on the Continent, there were the so-called sectarian groups, including the Anabaptists, Baptists, Congregationalists, Quakers, Mennonites, and scores of smaller groups. The first three Reformation movements were orthodox in our sense of the term. So, for the most part, were the sectarians. But in this latter group there were actual and potential threats to orthodoxy.

The sects broke with the other Reformation groups over the doctrine of the Church. For them, the Church was to consist only of the saints, that is, practicing and fully convinced Christians. They deplored the taking of babies into the Church by infant baptism, for only those who lived the Christian life ought to be in the Church, they believed.

Because the sectarians emphasized that each Church member should be a practicing Christian, they were suspicious of the doctrine of salvation by grace. They saw too many people who used the doctrine as an excuse for not living Christian lives. Their protest gained more cogency as the years passed, and the second generation of Reformation leaders began to interpret salvation by faith to mean salvation by belief. Instead of faith being the commitment of one's life to God, as it had been for Paul and Luther, it meant believing the orthodox creeds and doctrines. In their reaction against the abuses of such a system, the sectarians were willing to run the risk of falling into a new legalism. The teachings of Jesus became rules that had to be followed by anyone who would join the Church.

Many of these groups, led by the Quaker George Fox, had a doctrine of the inner inspiration of each man by the Holy Spirit, or Inner Light. There was nothing unorthodox about this, as Christians have always believed that the Holy Spirit speaks to the heart of man and guides him. Both Luther and Calvin laid a great emphasis upon it. But there was a tendency in sectarian circles to find the ultimate authority in the Inner Light rather than in the Bible. In time this led to a radical criticism of the Bible and orthodoxy.

By the year 1600 a radical Protestantism had arisen to attack orthodoxy. It was known as Socinianism after its founder Fausto Socinus, who fled to Poland to escape persecution both by Catholics and by Protestants. This movement was the forerunner of modern Unitarianism and modern liberalism. The Socinians accepted the Bible but not uncritically. They found many errors in it. They insisted that nothing can be the revelation of God which is against reason and common sense or which is morally useless. On this basis many biblical stories were discredited.

The orthodox doctrine of the Trinity was rejected because of the inadequacy of the Greek philosophical concepts which had been used in the writing of the creeds. It was denied that Jesus had a divine nature, although it was granted that he was a higher type of man, a superman, so to speak.

The doctrine of original sin was discarded as irrational. Man still has the same freedom to choose between good and evil that Adam had. A hereditary sin is contradictory; there is no sin without guilt, and if we are guilty before we are born we must have sinned before we were born, which is ridiculous.

The idea that Jesus could have borne the punishment for our guilt is immoral and absurd, insisted the Socinians. One man cannot be punished justly in place of another. God needs no such scheme, for he is willing to forgive freely when man turns to him.

The Socinian faith was reduced to what was felt to be the bare essentials. Socinians believed that God rewarded and punished men, in an afterlife, for their obedience or disobedience to the ethical law taught most clearly by Jesus. The Resurrection and other Bible miracles were the proofs that Jesus spoke with divine authority.

With the rise of rationalism, a new religious movement, Deism, came to the fore. The Socinians had been concerned to be Christian, but the Deists looked for a religion that would be common to all rational men of good will. The Deists were repelled by the religious wars of the seventeenth century and the heresy hunting of the age. One of its first thinkers, Lord Herbert of Cherbury (died 1648), argued that a rational religion must be independent of any special revelation. The first tenet of such a religion is God, who can be proved to exist by the fact that the world needs a creator. Since there is a God, he deserves to be adored and obeyed, which means that man must live ethically. When we fail to do this, we must repent and strive to overcome our sins. Since this life does not bring adequate reward for goodness and punishment for evil, there must be another life in which the accounts are settled.

The God of the Deists has sometimes been called the watchmaker God. God created the world as a watchmaker makes a watch, and then wound it up and let it run. Since

God was a perfect "watchmaker," there was no need of his interfering with the world later. Hence the Deists rejected anything that seemed to be an interference of God with the world, such as miracles or a special revelation through the Bible.

The Deists believed that their religion was the original religion of man. From it had come, by distortion, all other religions. These distortions were the work of priests who concocted the theologies, myths, and doctrines of the various religions in order to enhance their own power.

Deism never got down to the common man; it was a religion for intellectuals only. Its power among the intellectuals is attested by the influence that it had upon the writing of the Declaration of Independence in America. The critique which Kant made of the proofs of God was a more serious blow to the Deists than it was to the orthodox, for rational proof of God was far more central to the former than to the latter.

As the modern world began to become smaller, Christians had to face the fact that theirs was not the only religion in the world. Of course, this was not discovered for the first time. For centuries Europe had trembled in fear of Mohammedan conquest. But the day came when the Christian began to meet individuals from other religions; he began to read their literature and to digest the meaning of their faith. A new science, Comparative Religions, grew up to study non-Christian religions. This movement was spurred by Deism, with its faith in the simple universal religion that had originally been held by all men. Ironically, research into other religions broke down this Deist theory instead of supporting it.

Several disturbing facts for orthodoxy came from this new science. Parallels to many Christian beliefs, such as the Virgin Birth, were found among non-Christian religions. Every religion abounded in miracle stories, and if Christianity was proved true by miracles, as even the Socinians thought, what of the miracles in other faiths? Every religion had its sacred Scriptures, claiming to be revealed. Why then suppose that the Christian Scriptures are superior? Furthermore, men who were primarily interested in the ethical consequences of religion found that other religions also had high ethical teaching. In short, the uniqueness of Christianity was questioned and challenged.

Another important nineteenth century development was biblical criticism. The term "criticism" is somewhat misleading. It is not meant to imply tearing the Bible to pieces, although to many an orthodox Christian that is what seemed to be happening. Actually, the Bible critic is simply a scholar who studies the Bible to find its more exact meaning. He is critical in the sense that he tries to find rational or scientific reasons for his conclusions rather than to accept the dogmas of the Church. Albert Schweitzer points out that some of the first critics to contribute to our knowledge of the New Testament were enemies of Christ, men who looked at the Bible critically because they hoped to destroy the religion based upon it. But the Church quickly took Bible criticism into itself, and as time passed the seminaries became the centers of critical research. This was not achieved without a battle, but the critics slowly won their case, although many a scholar lost his position in the process.

Biblical criticism came to be expressed in two forms, the lower and higher criticism. The terms are purely technical and do not imply any value judgments. The lower critic dealt with problems of the text, and tried to weigh the merits of the great many manuscripts of the Bible which have been discovered in order that he might find the earliest and most reliable text of the Bible. The only aspects of lower criticism that were new in the modern world were the greater exactness with which ancient manuscripts could be dated and read and the greater abundance of ancient manuscripts which have been discovered. Lower critics did not produce anything which shook orthodoxy unduly.

Higher criticism begins where lower criticism leaves off. The higher critic is not primarily interested in the accuracy of the text; he is interested in the meaning of the words. He wishes to read between the lines and get behind the text to the events as they really happened. To do so, he must find out when each passage of Scripture was written, who wrote it, and to whom and why it was written. The higher critic believes that we can only understand the Bible if we can see it against this kind of background. For example, a Psalm takes on quite a different meaning when the critic concludes that it was not written by David, as tradition believed, but that it was a folk song that grew out of the sufferings of the Jews while they were in exile.

Higher criticism is no more of a modern discovery than lower. From the second century to the present we find Christian writers using a higher critical approach to enable them to understand the Bible. But in the modern period a new weapon came into the hands of the critic—that of historical criticism. This new method had been developed by the later Renaissance and was improved by students of history. It was applied first to the books of the ancient world, where it detected many forgeries and revised ideas of authorship in ancient manuscripts. In the nineteenth century this method was applied to the Bible as if the Bible were any other ancient book whose credentials had to pass the bar of historical method. This did result in many discoveries that shook orthodoxy.

Some of the results of higher criticism which alarmed orthodoxy may be quickly mentioned. Critics generally agreed that Moses did not write the first five books of the Bible, as had been believed. Instead they were written by at least four different writers. Among other things, this meant that we have two different stories of Creation in Genesis. Critics believed that books and passages which purport to tell the future had been written after the events which presumably they had forecast. It came to be generally accepted that the Gospel of John, long the favorite Gospel of the orthodox, was not written by the Apostle John and that it is not good history. The first three Gospels, called the Synoptics, were dated much earlier than John's and were considered more reliable. More important, however, than any of these details, was the fact that doubt was thrown upon the belief that the Bible is an infallible authority upon all things which it mentions.

One of the important developments of higher criticism was the search for the "historical Jesus." This term is interesting, for it implies that Jesus, as he lived in history, was different from the Jesus that we find portrayed in the Gospels. Critics tried to read between the lines and find out what Jesus had really been like. They assumed that the early Church and the Gospel writers had added many things to the biblical account so that the problem was to sift the authentic sayings and doings of Jesus from the later additions. Scores of lives of Jesus were written during the nineteenth century, each claiming that it portrayed the true Jesus. Two of the best known are *The Life of Jesus* by David Friedrich Strauss (1835–1836) and Renan's *The Life of Jesus* (1863). Although the various "lives" contradicted each other at many points, they did agree in removing the miraculous elements. They all assumed that science had proved miracles to be impossible, and they agreed that Jesus had not taught that he was the Messiah or that the world was coming to an end when he would return to set up the Kingdom of God. The *reductio ad absurdum* came when some of these critics decided that, since the Gospel records were so unreliable, there never was a Jesus at all. He was a myth invented by the early Church. This view was easily discredited, but it bothered many an orthodox thinker for a while.

Albert Schweitzer, in his book *The Quest of the Historical Jesus* (1906), has written a brilliant history of this epoch and reveals how most of the biographies of Jesus were simply the pictures of what the writers wanted to find. They did not describe Jesus, the Galilean carpenter of the first century, but a figure who taught and acted like a nineteenth century intellectual. Yet there was cold comfort for the orthodox in Schweitzer's book. Schweitzer found that Jesus did teach he was the Messiah and that he believed that the Kingdom of God was about to come down from heaven to remake the earth. The ethics which Jesus taught were simply the ethics for living during the short interval before he returned on the clouds of heaven to usher in a new day. Jesus went to his death in the rather pathetic illusion that by so doing he would hasten the coming of the Kingdom.

European Christianity met the challenge of these various developments by two schools of thought which, in turn, affected American thought. The first began with Friedrich Schleiermacher (1768–1834). He found that the prevailing rationalism of the eighteenth century had been replaced by the romanticism of the nineteenth. Where formerly cold reason had been the highest pursuit of man, now emotion and feeling moved into a prominent place. Against this background, Schleiermacher tried to rehabilitate religion among the intellectuals who had, for the most part, forsaken it during the eighteenth century.

Schleiermacher insisted that the great debates over proofs of God, the authority of Scriptures, miracles, and the like, were all on the outside fringe of religion. The heart of religion was and always had been feeling, not rational proofs and discussions. The God of religion is not, as much speculation seemed to imply, a theory dragged in to explain the universe. God, to the religious man, is an experience, a living reality. Religion is based on feeling or intuition. Schleiermacher analyzed this feeling in terms of dependence upon the universe. He pointed out that every man has to come to terms with the universe, the source of his being. All great art and literature has a concept of the totality of the universe, and this is, whether it is recognized or not, an experience of God. Unfortunately, this has been obscured by the traditional religionists. They have identified religion with creeds, and men who could no longer accept the creeds thought that they were through with religion. But this was a tragic mistake, for they still were in contact with God through their feeling of dependence upon the universe.

For Schleiermacher religion is essentially ethical because when one becomes aware of his dependence upon the universe he is immediately aware of his relationship with his fellow men, who are likewise bound to the source of their being. In all religions we find this primary experience of man, and it is expressed in various doctrines and forms. But if the forms become too important we must get rid of them in order that we can once more find the experience of religion in all of its purity and power.

Sin occurs when man tries to live by himself, isolated from the universe and his fellow men. He lives for his own selfish interest, but in so living he finds that he is miserable. This misery of man in his isolation is proof, to Schleiermacher, of man's oneness with God. It can be overcome only when one loses himself in the service of God and man.

Because sin separates man from God and his fellow man, God sends a mediator in Jesus Christ. The uniqueness of Christ is not to be found, for Schleiermacher, in some metaphysical doctrine about Jesus or in some miraculous origin such as the Virgin Birth. The real miracle is Jesus himself. In Jesus we find a man who had the sense of God-consciousness to a supreme degree; where we all have flashes of God, he had complete knowledge. Where we give fitful obedience, he gave complete obedience. Jesus, as the God-filled man, was a great pioneer in the realm of the spirit and morals.

Because Jesus has the full and complete knowledge of God, he is able to communicate consciousness of God to others. Through Jesus we can come into a vital and living relationship with God. The Church is the living witness to the fact that down through the centuries men have come to a vital God-consciousness through their contact with the life of Jesus. This leads to a true reunion with our fellow men in brotherly living.

In Schleiermacher religion found an answer to many of the problems of his age. For one thing, religion was made independent of philosophy and science. Religion, based on the individual's personal experience, had a realm of its own; it was its own proof; it bore its own validity. Furthermore, the center of religion is shifted from the Bible to the heart of the believer. Biblical criticism cannot harm Christianity, for the heart of the Bible message is that which it speaks to the individual, and it speaks even more clearly because the critics have enabled us to understand it.

Furthermore, other religions are no longer a problem; they too have their God-consciousness. The doctrines of religion may differ, but beneath them all there is the common experience. It is no wonder that Schleiermacher was hailed by many as the savior of religion, but much of his thought was obviously distasteful to orthodox Christianity.

Later in the nineteenth century, another school of thought began with another German thinker, Albrecht Ritschl (1822–1889). He was the great theologian of practicality. Religion must not be theoretical, he insisted. It must begin with the question, "What must I do to be saved?" but if that question means, "How can I go to heaven when I die?" then it is a theoretical question. To be saved means to live a new life, to be saved from sin, selfishness, fear, and guilt. Ritschl had no patience with metaphysics or with theological discussions that did not appear to him to have practical consequences. For example, he threw out Augustine's doctrine of original sin because it did not seem to him to deal with the practical question raised by the fact that some men are more sinful than others.

To be practical, Christianity must be built upon fact, so Ritschl welcomed the search for the historical Jesus. The great Christian fact is the impact that Jesus has made upon the Church through the centuries. God is not to be found in nature, which is red in tooth and claw and speaks ambiguously of its Creator. We find God instead in history, where movements arise dedicated to the values that make life meaningful. The task of theology is to turn men again to Jesus and remind them anew of what it means to follow him.

For Ritschl religion is based on value judgments and is to be sharply separated from science. Science tells us the facts, things as they are; but religion weighs the facts and deems some more valuable than others. The great fact about man is that, although he is a product of nature and evolution, he has a sense of values. We can explain this only if we interpret the universe as one which creates not only atoms and molecules but also values. For Ritschl God is not known intuitively, as for Schleiermacher, nor is God known by a rational inference from the world, as for the Deists. Instead,

God is the necessary postulate to explain the sense of worth that man has.

Conflict between science and religion begins either when religion tries to make statements of fact or when science tries to make value judgments. When religion makes statements of fact, such as proclaiming that the evolutionary theory is wrong, the result is simply poor science. When science makes value judgments, such as saying that because man has evolved from the lower animals he is worth no more than the animals, the result is poor religion. Of course, Ritschl did not mean that science and religion should go off into two separate rooms and never speak to each other. Quite the contrary, the same man was to be both scientific and religious; religion was to use the facts of science, and science was to cherish the value judgments of religion. But it should be clear that religion and science are two basically different approaches to reality.

Applied to the problem of biblical criticism, this approach of Ritschl was very helpful to many in his generation. Biblical criticism takes the way of science; it decides what are the facts about authorship, date, and meaning of the biblical books. This is vital, for religion must be based upon fact. But the facts are not religion until they have been evaluated, and this cannot be performed by scientific criticism. If biblical criticism denies the occurrence of Jesus' miracles, his Virgin Birth, his preexistence, this does not make Jesus less valuable to us. Belief in the divinity of Jesus does not rest in any of these; it rests solely on the fact that he is the source of a value-creating movement; he has led men to find the God of values. That is, Jesus' life was the embodiment of such high ethical ideals and attainment that we are inspired to live as he did. Jesus is divine in the sense that he can do for us what God does; he makes us conscious of the highest in life. From Jesus' influence comes the Church, a value-creating community —the spearhead for building a society inspired by love, the Kingdom of God upon earth.

The man who did most to popularize Ritschl's views was Adolf von Harnack, a competent theologian in his own right and not simply the transmitter of another's views. His book *What Is Christianity?* (1901) was a record best seller. One of the reasons for its popularity was that it simplified Christianity. Harnack reduced Christianity to three affirmations. First, it affirmed belief in God the Father, his providence and goodness. Second, it affirmed faith in the divine sonship of man. Third, it affirmed faith in the infinite value of the human soul. He denied the miracles of Jesus and insisted that Jesus did not claim to be the Messiah or divine. It was Paul and later Greek thought that perverted Jesus' simple Gospel into the elaborate theology about Jesus that we find in later creeds. Hence the slogan that we must get back to the religion of Jesus, not the religion about Jesus.

The influence of Schleiermacher and Ritschl reached America late in the nineteenth century. Together they became the background of American liberalism. There had been prepared in America a movement to which these theologies could speak. From the time of Jonathan Edwards, America had begun to question the Calvinistic form of orthodoxy with which the country began. By the nineteenth century the Unitarian movement was active. It denied the Trinity, the divinity of Jesus, and had staked religion to the findings of man's reason and faith in man's essential goodness.

Horace Bushnell, a Congregationalist, had criticized the orthodox doctrines of the atonement and popularized the idea of growing into Christianity. For many, the idea that one could become a Christian by training from childhood, instead of undergoing a soul-shaking conversion at some point in life, implied that there was no original sin. The child was born naturally good and would stay that way if raised properly.

Modern liberalism in America is the result of the various forces discussed in this chapter, joining with the native American forms of liberal thought.

From this chapter it is clear that by the close of the nineteenth century orthodoxy was "sore opprest" and "by schisms rent asunder." And, when speaking of the history of thought, we must not forget that the nineteenth century ends in 1914, not 1900. If we might describe the situation in the terminology of the boxing ring, we might picture it thus: At the close of the round, orthodoxy was hanging on the ropes and the crowd was cheering for the knockout. But orthodoxy was saved by the bell (the First World War) and when the next round opened it came out fighting, with new vigor. Instead of retreating, it began to attack. It is still too early to decide if this new vigor is a permanent recovery or if it is a last desperate effort. But one thing is certain, orthodoxy has won the last couple of rounds on points and for the moment the crowd is with it. But this is the story of modern Christian thought.

CHAPTER 3

Fundamentalism or Conservative Christianity: The Defense of Orthodoxy

Most Americans are familiar with the term "fundamentalist" and many remember the theological battle early in this century between the fundamentalists and the liberals or modernists. All over the country, and in nearly every major denomination, there rose up men who were determined to protect the faith. To these dedicated men it was evident that the Christian Church had been infiltrated by subversives who would destroy Christianity from within.

The battle raged in Church assemblies, theological institutions, and the daily press. Young men about to be ordained to the ministry had to face a barrage of questions about their stand on the Virgin Birth, the bodily resurrection of Christ, blood atonement, and the infallibility of the Bible. We catch something of the flavor of the times in the following passage from an article in a secular magazine:

"A few years ago we couldn't have imagined the United States eagerly awaiting the news from some church convention. There wasn't any news in a church convention. . . .

the break came suddenly, about two years ago. What had happened no one seems to know; but the Virgin Birth presently began to run neck and neck with murder and politics for front page layouts, even in such newspapers as the *New York Times.* Ever since then religion has been the livest news there is.

"A few years ago the country waited eagerly while the Presbyterians, assembled in Columbus, Ohio, actually took a ballot on the Virgin Birth. A little later the Associated Press and all the other news agencies of the nation were covering in World Series, play-by-play fashion an argument in a Tennessee courtroom on the all-important problem of where Cain's wife came from and whether God could have worked by the day before he invented the sun.

"Now all eyes are beginning to turn toward New Orleans. The question at issue there is: Can a bishop think? Nobody seems to care particularly how the question is decided. The public isn't partisan; it is just eager for the news. For religion is news today, and no mistake."[1]

The term "fundamentalist" seems to have been used first by Dr. C. C. Laws, editor of the Baptist *Watchman-Examiner.* It implied that this view expressed the fundamentals of the Christian faith, the irreducible minimum of belief without which one could not be Christian. Many representatives of this school were unhappy about the title, preferring the term "conservative Christianity" or even just "Christianity." John Gresham Machen complained that he saw no reason why that

[1] Charles E. Wood, "Religion Becomes News," *The Nation,* Vol. 121, August 19, 1925, p. 204.

which had been known through history quite simply as Christianity should suddenly become another "ism."

The fundamentalist or conservative movement is not as easy to define as it seems at first glance. Usually it implies one who believes in the verbal inspiration of the Bible, that is, the belief that the words of the Bible are the direct and errorless words of God. Yet, on closer inspection, it becomes clear that the conservative is by no means primarily interested in taking the Bible as the literal, infallible word of God. His primary interest is in the preservation of orthodox Christianity, and he has chosen to make the doctrine of the errorless Scripture his first line of defense.

Paul Tillich has pointed out that whenever a movement is under attack, it tends to narrow itself. It retires within what it hopes to be an impenetrable fortress and battles, not only the invader from without, but also the subversive within. Today in America we see this development as America faces the threat of totalitarian Communism. America has narrowed itself. The subversives are being rooted out, and all those whose ideas differ from the norm are under suspicion and threat. It is precisely this principle that can enable us to understand fundamentalism. Fundamentalism is the response of a certain group of orthodox Christians to the challenge that we portrayed in the last chapter. To meet the challenge, fundamentalism aims to rid the Church of all who might give any comfort to the enemy. It narrows itself down to the area which it chooses to defend and makes revelation its front-line defense.

In our discussion of orthodoxy, we had little to say about the doctrine of revelation, that is, the doctrine of how God makes himself known to man. That is because there is no such orthodox doctrine in the sense in which there is an orthodox doctrine of the Trinity. There is in all orthodoxy the faith that God has revealed himself, particularly in the events recorded in the Bible. This special revelation begins with the choosing of the Jews and culminates in the man Jesus. But there has been no final agreement on how God is revealed in the Bible or in what form it is an inspired book. In fact, these are questions which did not become burning issues until the twentieth century.

In the pre-Reformation Church there were differences of opinion without any sharp conflict. Men like Augustine valued some parts of the Bible more than others, implying that there was a standard by which to test revelation within the Bible itself. Some thinkers, like Origen, interpreted the Bible allegorically, paying little attention to the literal meaning of its passages. Others, like Occam, had quite a literalistic point of view, the Bible being for them a divinely dictated law.

One of the most radical aspects of Luther's thinking was his handling of the Bible. He called Protestants back to the authority of the Bible over against the authority of the pope and the Church. In the light of this we can really appreciate the prophetic daring with which he treated the Bible. For Luther the Bible was not literally true from cover to cover nor were all parts of equal value. He found that there was a criterion within the Bible itself by which the whole could be judged. That criterion was the message of salvation by grace through faith which is spoken through Jesus Christ to the heart of the believer. The believer thus becomes a critic of the Bible. The Bible is a true revelation where, and only where, it speaks to this truth which man has found to be true in his life. In the light of this, Luther threw out completely the so-called Apocryphal books which are still in Catholic Bibles. He would have thrown out the books of Esther and Revelation also, but his followers balked. He did not place much value on James's Epistle. He recognized that many of the forecasts of the prophets were in error, so that the Bible was by no means infallibly correct in all details. He even conceded that another New Testament could be written if anyone were as completely dedicated to the Holy Spirit as were the biblical writers.

These were brave attitudes in Luther, and it is not surprising to find that his followers and even Luther himself often retreated from them. As time passed, the Protestants felt more and more need of authority. Rome boasted that it had one voice of unquestionable authority while Protestantism had many conflicting voices. The sixteenth and seventeenth centuries were centuries of authoritarianism; the authorities of the divine-right kings clashed with one another and with the authority of an infallible pope. It is not difficult to understand why Protestants met authority with authority, and when Protestants used authority it had to be the authority of the Bible. But if the Bible is the authority by which you vanquish king and pope, you cannot treat the Bible as freely as did Luther. To protect their authority the Protestants claimed that the Bible was the only infallible authority and, unlike that of pope and king, the literal word of God. Every word in the Bible was, they claimed, dictated by God to the men who wrote it. One Protestant,

A. Polanus, went so far as to insist that even the punctuation of the Bible was inspired and hence without error. It is this tradition which was inherited by fundamentalism.

To the fundamentalist this doctrine became the first defense against error. If one began by doubting any statement of the Bible, he had started down the slippery slope that, the fundamentalist believed, would lead to the denial of God and the divinity of Jesus, the loss of certainty of salvation, and finally the loss of ethics. The fundamentalist sees a "creeping humanism," the creeping in of ideas that will finally leave man without God, religion, or morality. The fact that people have appeared in the modern world who are without God, religion, or morality spurred the fundamentalist in his zeal to protect the doctrine of the infallible Bible.

The heart of fundamentalism is in its concern for salvation. The only really important question is, "Have you been saved?" Because man is helpless to save himself, God must act. This helplessness is due to the fall of Adam, which caused sin in the world, a sin that is inherited by all men. Man is born with the guilt of Adam upon his soul, and he has a flaw in his character which leads him to sin. This sinful creature can do no act which can please God and is hence doomed to everlasting punishment in Hell unless God does something for him.

God is a God of love, mercy, and justice. The liberals, says the fundamentalist, overlook God's judgment and thus the love of God becomes pure sentimentality in their teaching. It would be unjust for God to forgive sins lightly and let bygones be bygones while the consequences of a man's sin live on and continue to injure others. Man has sinned and, in a moral universe, he ought to pay for his sin. Therefore, in his love and mercy, God sent his only begotten Son into the world. Jesus led a sinless life and did not deserve to die, but he voluntarily accepted death in order that he might save men. His death becomes a substitutionary atonement. He suffered the penalties of man's sin in order that the justice of God might be appeased and man allowed to go free. Jesus' blood was shed to wash away man's sin just as, in the Old Testament, the blood of animals was shed in the sacrificial rituals. The death of Christ does not save a man, however, unless he accepts Christ as the Son of God. The man who accepts Christ is assured of heaven and receives the grace of God as a power that enables him to overcome sin in his earthly life.

The miracles are the seals by which God proved his activity and presence to men. We know that Jesus was the Son of God because he was born of a Virgin, healed the sick, raised the dead, and was raised from the dead himself in a bodily form.

Most fundamentalists believe in the doctrine of the "premillennial" coming of Christ. This doctrine teaches that the Kingdom of God is not here now in the Church, as some groups have believed, nor is it a perfect society that man can build upon earth as many liberals believe. The Kingdom of God, the perfect society, awaits the Second Coming of Christ, when he will return upon the clouds and when history will end in catastrophe. Christ, having judged the living and the risen dead, will set up his Kingdom and rule for a thousand years, the millennium. At the end of that period there will be a final battle between the forces of God and Satan, and in the victory of God all the saints will be elevated to heaven for eternity while the damned will writhe in Hell.

This is God's plan of salvation, but how do we know that it is true? We certainly cannot know it if any man tells us, for no man's word is able to give us the assurance of salvation. Only God can say if it is true or not. If the Bible is the word of man, then we are still in our sins, without the assurance of salvation. But if the Bible is the Word of God, unclouded by errors or opinions of man, then we have an absolute assurance. Thus the doctrine of the infallible Bible is the protection for the Gospel message.

The doctrine of the infallibility of the Bible is frequently misunderstood by those outside fundamentalism. One hears it confidently refuted by the charge that it is a doctrine of mechanical inspiration and killing literalism. Again, it is refuted by pointing out that we have many manuscripts of the Bible and that often these differ from one another in the wording of certain passages. If, however, we stop to remember that John Machen was one of the finest biblical scholars in America, we should realize that the scholarly conservative has an answer to such obvious criticism.

Machen and like-minded conservatives assert that only the original manuscript of the Bible, as first dictated by God, was free from error. They make no claim that any edition of the Bible which we have today is without error. In fact, these fundamentalists have done much work in biblical scholarship to restore the best text of the Bible. Although fanatical fundamentalists, believing the King James Version of the Bible to be infallible, have burnt the Revised Standard Version, many other fundamentalists have advised their people to read the Revised Version. These fundamentalists believe that the original text of the Bible which was free from error has been lost because God knew that man would worship it as he has worshiped other religious relics. The men who copied the Bible made errors, which explains the differences in the manuscripts of the Bible, but God kept them from the kind of errors that would have hindered salvation. E. J. Carnell quotes the Introduction to the Revised Standard New Testament, in which a group of non-fundamentalist scholars concede that no manuscripts have been found that would change any doctrine of the Christian faith. This, says Carnell, is all that any conservative needs.

Furthermore, it is unfair to charge the fundamentalist with being a literalist. He is not required to lop off his right hand or pluck out his eye because Jesus told men to do this. The fundamentalist understands that the Bible sometimes speaks in poetic or allegorical language. He does not follow the literal words of Scripture; he follows the "natural" meaning. Where the Bible obviously means to be taken literally, he does so. Thus he believes in the bodily resurrection of Jesus because one cannot read the accounts without realizing that they say quite literally that Jesus arose in his body. But the fundamentalist is not required to suppose that Isaiah saw the hills leaping and clapping their hands. The inspired word of God may be poetry as well as prose, and as such it is to be interpreted in its natural sense.

Having made such concessions, it may seem that the fundamentalist is not so different from the liberal. The basic difference, however, is found when we consider the reaction to higher criticism. The lower criticism of the Bible is an area in which the fundamentalist gladly works. In fact, he has greater concern than the liberal in finding the manuscripts that take us back most closely to the original version of the Bible.

Higher criticism is, however, a different matter. The higher critic applies to the Bible those methods which have proved successful in dealing with other ancient writings. Here, says the fundamentalist, the higher critic shows the weakness of his position. He has presupposed, either implicitly or explicitly, that the Bible is just another ancient book and that it does not require a special method to be understood. Since he has refused to take the Bible upon its own terms as a supernatural revelation, he quite naturally misses the whole point. The higher critic, charges the fundamentalist, assumes that his reason is sufficient to know all that one needs to know in order to understand the world. This is a presupposition that makes revelation unnecessary.

Because the higher critic has a presupposition, unproved and sometimes unconscious, he searches for the naturalistic causes of the Bible and in the process distorts the Bible, insists the fundamentalist. If Isaiah speaks about Cyrus, it must mean, the critic feels, that that section of Isaiah was written after the time of Cyrus because the critic refuses to believe in the possibility of anyone foretelling future events. So the critic invents, from his fertile imagination, a Second Isaiah to account for this section of the book of Isaiah. Acting upon the same principle, he gives later dates to various books, and where he cannot do so he assumes that the passage has been tampered with by later writers. He is not deterred by the fact that the truly scientific method of lower criticism has not found any manuscript which would bear out his theory of tampering.

The same is true of the miracle stories. The higher critic has not disproved the possibility of miracles, believes the fundamentalist; he has not analyzed the biblical narratives and found them self-contradictory or innately irrational. But the critic has no room for miracles in his world view; they are distasteful to him. So again he turns his imagination loose and works out ingenious theories to explain what really happened in place of the miracle. His attitude is neither critical nor scientific; it is based upon a dogmatic faith. Here it is the fundamentalist who is scientific, for he does not, like the critic, presuppose that miracles are impossible. He looks at the facts with an open mind and finds evidence that miracles have happened.

In short, as the fundamentalist sees it, what divides him from the higher critic is not that one believes and the other doubts that Moses wrote the first five books of the Bible. Nor is the difference that one accepts the Bible as reliable history and the other questions it. In fact, there is room among fundamentalists for some variation on these points. The real difference lies in two totally different world views. The higher critic, charges the fundamentalist, assumes that the world is a self-contained unity that can be fully comprehended by man's intellect. He has no room for special revelation or for anything that might be called the interference of God with his creation. In short, he denies the reality of the supernatural; nature is all and explains all. The fundamentalist accepts the reality of the supernatural God and of

God's supernatural intervention among men. The world owes its very being to the fact of God's creation. If the Creator chooses to act with his creative power again within the world to give a special revelation of himself or to perform miracles, then the truly reasonable man will accept this fact and not close his mind to it.

Another misconception of fundamentalism lies in the tendency to call it an irrational movement. It would be more correct to term fundamentalism as rationalism within Christianity. No religious movement lays more emphasis upon a rational faith than it. The defenders of fundamentalism have continually taken their case into the arena of logic and reason and have felt that it was precisely there that they had the best case. E. J. Carnell, in his book *An Introduction to Christian Apologetics*, spends 350 pages in presenting a closely reasoned argument, tested by coherency and ability to explain the facts. He reveals a knowledge of modern philosophy, science, and non-fundamentalist theology. He attacks every effort to shield religion from the responsibility of defending itself rationally. He will not allow it to hide behind the intuitions of mysticism or feeling with Schleiermacher, nor will he allow it to express itself in the contradictory paradoxes of Karl Barth. He has only one reason for accepting conservative Christianity: it explains all of the facts of existence more coherently than any alternative philosophy. One may not agree with the arguments of this book, but one cannot call it obscurantist or irrational.

Although Carnell represents contemporary fundamentalism, his intellectual fathers had the same love of reason. Machen, writing during the twenties, defended fundamentalism against the liberals because he found it more rational. In fact, as Machen saw it, the great weakness of liberalism was its irrationalism and anti-intellectualism.

Liberals, said Machen, argue that religion is an inexpressible experience, that the intellectual expression of it can be only symbolic, and that thus theologies may vary while the experience remains the same. So, says Machen, the best way to make oneself unpopular in theology is to demand that people define the terms they use so blithely. Liberals toss around words like "God," "atonement," "redemption," and "Christianity," but refuse to define them so that they will mean the same thing for all people.

Liberals are obscurantists because they disparage the teaching of doctrine. The liberal says that he is only interested in applying Christianity to life. But, asks Machen, how can you apply something unless you know what it is? Yet, to know what Christianity is, you have to think about it; you have to consider its doctrines; in short, you need the theology which the liberal boasts that he ignores. This liberal disdain for theology is an excuse for shallow thinking or, worse still, for no thinking.

Furthermore, charged Machen, the liberal is anti-intellectual because of his habit of reading into the Bible what he wants to find there rather than seeing what really is there. The "Jesus of history" about which the liberal speaks a great deal is not the Jesus who is plainly evident in the Gospels, but the Jesus whom the liberals would like to find. The liberal wants a Jesus who is only a man and not the Son of God, and at the same time he accepts Jesus as the greatest moral and religious teacher. Could anything be more illogical? If Jesus was not and is not the Son of God, insists Machen, then he is the very reverse of a reliable teacher of ethics. For Jesus claimed to be divine; he claimed to have authority over men; he claimed to do that which only God can do—forgive sins; he claimed to be the Messiah, foretelling that he would return on the clouds of heaven; he asserted that he was the Way, the Truth, and the Life. If Jesus were only a man and claimed these things, he cannot be our example, for he was either a madman or a charlatan. Either way, it is irrational to honor him as a great ethical teacher. Yet this is typical of the failure of the liberal to be rational, to face the facts as they are and not as he would like them to be.

In short, at the time when liberals were hailing themselves as the defenders of reason and of rational religion, this scholarly fundamentalist arose to charge that it is liberalism which has betrayed reason. One may argue that there are flaws in the details of the fundamentalist's argument, that he takes all the mystery out of religion and makes it prosaically rational, but one cannot argue that fundamentalism is an irrational system.

Many people will react against the idea that fundamentalism is a rational system because they cannot forget the great battle waged by fundamentalists against the doctrine of evolution. In what sense, it will be asked, can any movement be called rational if it denies the facts and findings of science? Men still recall the infamous Scopes trial when the teaching of evolution was banned in Tennessee. We must remember, however, that fundamentalism as a system can no more be justly judged by what its fanatics do than America can be justly judged by what every irresponsible tourist does. Whatever may be the case in the backwoods, the intellectual leaders of fundamentalism have never rested their case against evolution upon the blind acceptance of biblical quotations. In William Jennings Bryan's book *In His Image*, one finds a rational criticism of evolution and not a dogmatic denial of it on the basis of proof texts. In fact, science has come to accept some of the points made by Bryan.

Furthermore, fundamentalists like Carnell are willing to accept evolution. Carnell has a theory which he calls "Threshold Evolution" that harmonizes the Bible and evolutionary theories. Carnell points out that the Bible does not say that God created each individual species in the form that we know it today. Rather, God created each creature "after their kind," such as "herbs yielding seed" or "creeping things." Within each "kind" there are numerous species and these may have evolved from out of the basic "kind." What science cannot show is that one "kind" ever evolves from another. Here biology talks of its missing links or mutations, but it has no definite facts to work with. This "Threshold Evolution" can explain all of the facts known to science as adequately as any alternative theory. It enables the fundamentalist to believe that man is the result of a special creation of God and that he did not evolve from lesser animals, for humans were one of the originally created "kinds."

Before supposing that fundamentalists are all anti-scientific, we must mention the fact that many fundamentalists are scientists. The fundamentalist Inter-Varsity Christian Fellowship never lacks for accredited scientists. I have heard speakers at its meetings who were on the faculties of some of the best medical colleges in the country, and a well known professor of archaeology from a leading educational institution. There is a group of scientists organized into the American Science Affiliation, which requires a doctorate degree in some science before a man can become a member. Its members pledge themselves to the faith that true science and the infallible Bible cannot contradict each other. Several writings have come from this group to prove their point.

During the first twenty-five years of the century, the fundamentalists were active in most Protestant denominations. They were on the offensive and attempted to root all liberals out of Church offices. Successful attacks were made on professors in theological seminaries, upon students who were about to be ordained, and even upon ordained clergymen. One of the better known cases involved Harry Emerson Fosdick, who was forced to leave the Presbyterian Church and return to his own denomination, the Baptist.

Fundamentalists were apprehensive of the charge that they were narrow-minded opponents of free speech, and Machen answered it. Again he turned the liberal charge against the liberal. Narrow-mindedness, he insisted, does not consist in devotion to certain convictions or in rejection of others. That man is narrow-minded who rejects another man's convictions without trying to understand them. The liberal is continually saying, "Let us be broadminded and unite in the same churches, for our doctrinal differences are mere trifles." But, points out Machen, it is the very essence of conservative Christianity to regard doctrinal issues as matters of supreme importance. It is not narrow-minded either to believe or to reject the doctrine of the substitutionary death of Jesus for our sins. But it is the height of narrow-mindedness to ask, as the liberal asks, that a man who believes it should pretend that it is a trifle. If the liberal were truly broadminded, that is, if he truly tried to understand the other's position and appreciate it even if he could not agree with it, then he would see that his plea for union is a plea for union upon the liberal's terms. The liberal is, in effect, asking for unconditional surrender on the part of the conservative.

On the question of free speech, Machen argues that he has no desire that the liberal should not be free to hold and to spread his opinions. In fact, Machen concedes, the liberal may be a better Christian in the eyes of God than the fundamentalist, but only God can know that. Nevertheless, insists Machen, the Christian Churches do have their creeds. A liberal may not agree with them; that is his right and privilege. He may think the creeds wrong or he may think that it is wrong to have any kind of creed. But if this is the case, honesty demands that the liberal go elsewhere to spread his views. Why does he ask to be supported by a Church with which he disagrees? How can he honestly ask that a Church support him while he undermines the doctrines on which the Church is built?

Again the political analogy comes to mind. Today many people would argue, in a way that reminds us of Machen, that Communists may have a right to hold their opinions. But they do not have a right to hold responsible governmental or teaching positions which they would use to undermine the Constitution upon which the country is founded. Once more we find evidence that fundamentalism can be understood as a threatened movement, a movement which has to tighten its lines for defense.

As time passed, liberals began to win more and more of the battles. The leading seminaries became the centers of liberalism, and fundamentalists either withdrew in discomfort or, upon retirement, were replaced by liberals. In a sense, if you want a date for the end of the fundamentalist-liberal controversy, it came in 1929. In that year Machen failed in his opposition to a reorganization of Princeton Seminary, where he taught. As a result, he resigned and helped to found Westminster Seminary in Philadelphia. A second defeat came for Machen when he and other conservative Presbyterians founded an independent mission board. The Presbyterian Church ordered the dismantling of the organization, and the order was fought through the Church courts. Finally, in 1936 the General Assembly ruled against the independent board, and when its members refused to obey they were expelled. Machen and the others founded a new denomination for themselves, the Presbyterian Church of America. These events are evidence of the fact that by the thirties it was the fundamentalists, not the liberals, who were finding it necessary to leave Churches and seminaries.

When one speaks of the end of the fundamentalist-liberal controversy, it does not mean that the fundamentalists disappeared. It does mean that the active battle died away. By the end of the thirties the liberals, as we shall see, were fighting for their lives on another front and had no time for continuing the battle with the fundamentalists. The pattern had been set so that liberals were found in one congregation and fundamentalists in another. Frequently, separate seminaries, one liberal and one fundamentalist, supplied ministers to the congregations even when they were of the same denomination. A large number of fundamentalists found their spiritual home among the smaller sects where, unrestrained by scholarship, they became lost in a maze of esoteric emotional extravagances. Several of these groups have banded into the American Council of Christian Churches, which periodically makes headlines by calling the National Council of Churches a Communist front.

The end of the controversy may be called a truce rather than a peace. Theologians of the two groups ignore each other. It is the parish minister, rather than the theologian, who must carry on the struggle today.

The present situation may not prove stable. With non-fundamentalists coming to a new appreciation of orthodoxy and a new group of conservatives arising, there are evidences that the groups are once more approaching a position where they may at least have enough in common to engage once more in an exchange of ideas. Furthermore, a new theological generation is arising that no longer has conditioned responses to members of the other group.

E. J. Carnell is typical of the new fundamentalism. Carnell, professor of Apologetics at Fuller Theological Seminary, is a graduate of Wheaton College and Westminster Theological Seminary, both strongholds of conservative Christianity. He took his doctoral degree, however, from Harvard Divinity School, a strong outpost of liberalism. He has joined both the American Philosophical Association and the National Association of Biblical Instructors, neither of which can be suspected of fundamentalism. He has written a book on the theology of Reinhold Niebuhr and, as mentioned earlier, he wrote a book which makes a rational and philosophical defense of conservative Christianity. The non-fundamentalist world cannot justify itself in ignoring a man of his stature.

A sign of the times may be an editorial by Chad Walsh which appeared in the Sept. 6, 1953, issue of *Episcopal Church News*. He pointed out that fundamentalists are taking note of the development of thought in the Anglican tradition. The time, he suggests, may have come to begin anew the interchange of ideas between fundamentalist and non-fundamentalist Christians.

Although fundamentalism is associated in many people's minds with snake handling, Holy Rollers, and fanaticism in general, it is in reality the faith by which many millions of our citizens live. It is a simple faith, yet full of comfort and inspiration. It has a democratic appeal, for each child of God may turn to the Bible where he can read and understand without having to follow the dictates of the supermen, the biblical critics. In this faith the common man finds a sense of dignity and worth. Regardless of his station in life, he has the assurance that he is a ransomed son of God. In his neighbor he sees a fellow sinner to whom he may stretch his hand in Christian love. This faith moved men to abolish slavery; it is the faith that went west with the pioneers. Today its adherents give more of their time and money to charity and the promotion of their religion than do those of any alternate position. We may well ponder about the glow of faith that shines in the face of the man who sings, "Give me that old-time religion." In a world of change and upheaval, here is a force that draws upon the treasures of the past. It has something to teach us all.

CHAPTER 4

Liberalism: The Remaking of Orthodoxy

The term "liberalism," or "modernism," is difficult to define. For one thing, it became popular during the days of the fundamentalist-liberal conflict when anyone who was not a fundamentalist was, by definition, a liberal or a modernist. The latter two terms are used synonymously despite attempts to distinguish them. A further problem with definition is that liberalism is, by its very nature, such that there will be within it a great many diverse positions.

Despite the varieties of liberalism it did mean, for the majority of its defenders in the early years of this century, a reconstruction of orthodox Christianity. Although the fundamentalists saw the liberals as subversives of the faith, liberals saw themselves as the saviors of the essence of Christianity. For the liberal, it was the fundamentalist who was destroying Christianity by forcing it into the molds of the past and making it impossible for any intelligent man to hold it. Typical of the attitude of liberals was the oft-quoted statement of Fosdick that, for him, it was not a question of new theology or old but a question of new theology or no theology.

If we are to understand liberalism we must realize that it

has two elements. There is first of all the method of liberalism, a method that means liberals probably will come to somewhat different conclusions. There is, in addition, a body of thought which has grown up as typical of liberals.

The method of liberalism includes the attempt to modernize Christian theology. The world, liberals argue, has changed radically since the early creeds of Christendom were formulated; this makes the creeds sound archaic and unreal to the modern man. We have to rethink Christianity in thought forms which the modern world can comprehend. Fosdick argued that we must express the essence of Christianity, its "abiding experiences," but that we must not identify these with the "changing categories" in which they have been expressed in the past. For example, says Fosdick, an abiding experience of Christianity has been its conviction that God will triumph over evil. This has been traditionally pictured in the category of Christ's Second Coming on the clouds to destroy evil and set up the good. We can no longer retain this outworn category but we can still believe the truth which this ancient thought form was trying to express. We can continue to work in the faith that, through his devoted followers, God is now building his Kingdom and that there will be a renewing of our life, individual and social, to bring it into conformity with the will of God. The essence of the faith is thus retained, argues Fosdick, while the thought form in which it was once clothed has been abandoned.

A second aspect of the method of liberalism is its refusal to accept religious belief on authority alone. Instead, it insists that all beliefs must pass the bar of reason and experience. Man's mind is capable of thinking God's thoughts after him. Man's intuitions and reason are the best clues that we have to the nature of God. The mind must be kept open to all truth, regardless of whence it comes. This means that the liberal must have an open mind; no questions are closed. New facts may change the convictions that have become hallowed by custom and time. The liberal will venture forth into the unknown, firmly believing that all truth must be God's truth. In this spirit, the liberal accepts the higher criticism of the Bible and the theory of evolution. He refuses to have a religion that is afraid of truth or that tries to protect itself from critical examination.

It is evident that in so far as a man is a liberal on the basis of his method, it is possible to have liberals who draw diametrically opposed conclusions. It is not unimaginable that a man might follow the liberal method and come to a very conservative theological position. But liberalism came to be associated with certain conclusions as well as with the method described, and to continue our analysis of liberalism we must examine some of these.

Behind liberalism as it grew early in this century lay the philosophy of Absolute Idealism, coming from Hegel and Lotze but reinterpreted for America by Josiah Royce. Idealism is based on the belief that, if man is to have any faith in his knowledge, he must presuppose a rational structure to the world apart from his mind. Man's reasoning powers, his logic and his a priori assumptions can only understand the world if the world acts in accordance with them. In other words, we can only trust our minds if the world is ultimately based on mind or reason. Idealism thus came to interpret all reality as the manifestation of a divine mind. Idealism seemed very appealing to many Christians because it attacked all philosophies of materialism.

Idealists like Royce and Hegel had made Christian terminology an inherent part of their systems. But to these men the Christian doctrines were only symbols of rational truths known to man's reason. Thus the divinity of Jesus was a symbolic statement for the fact that all men have a divine aspect to their natures. The basic concept of the Bible, which is that God has revealed himself in certain events of history, was considered by the idealists as naïve and pre-philosophical.

Idealism was an optimistic philosophy. It believed that the world was inherently rational and that reason was slowly overcoming the irrational. Good, it believed, was more basic than evil, so that the victory of goodness was ultimately assured. Sometimes this was identified with Christian belief in the Kingdom of God or, as Royce called it, the "Beloved Community."

Liberalism seldom capitulated completely to idealistic philosophy because the liberal theologians could not forget the Bible. But the liberals did draw heavily upon idealistic thinking. One of the most important ideas drawn from idealism was that of the immanence of God. Here we must examine some technical theological terms—"immanence" and "transcendence." Immanence implies an idea of God dwelling in the world and working through nature. Extreme immanence is pantheism, which says that God is the world and the world is God. Such pantheism appears in several of the idealistic philosophers but is rare among the liberals.

Transcendence implies the reality of God apart from the world. Extreme transcendence is found in the Deists, for whom God is as separate from the world as the watchmaker is from his watch.

It is obvious that fundamentalism emphasizes transcendence without completely denying immanence. Its God is distinct from the world, and when he enters the world he comes in the form of miracle and special acts of revelation. Over against this, liberalism insists upon finding God in the whole of life and not in just a few spectacular events. God's way of doing things is the way of progressive change and natural law. Liberalism denies that some things are caused by natural forces and others by supernatural forces. The liberal sees God working in and through all that happens or is. Thus the Virgin Birth is important to fundamentalists as proof that in Christ the supernatural is at work. For the liberal the Virgin Birth is not only unnecessary but an embarrassment, for he finds God at work in the birth of every child.

Despite this emphasis upon immanence, most liberals retained the belief that God was transcendent as well as immanent. For example, Rufus Jones, in a passage which argues for the immanence of God, goes on to say that God is spirit and that it is the essence of spirit, even in the form in which we find it in man, to transcend itself. Therefore an immanent spiritual God must transcend the space-time universe. He is more than the universe but he is not radically separated from it.

In view of its belief in the immanent God, it is clear that liberalism would find the theory of evolution not simply a bitter pill to be swallowed by men who were determined to face all truth, but rather a vindication of the immanent view of God. Instead of suddenly breaking through the clouds to create the world, God had been working for ages slowly building through natural law the universe as we find it today. Most liberals would agree with the poet who said, "Some call it evolution, and others call it God."

Since God is at work in the world, and particularly at work in the spiritual life of man, God becomes, in liberalism, a humanized God. This does not mean that God becomes a glorified human being or that man becomes God, but it does mean that God is required to have the spiritual characteristics which we consider good in man. One liberal put it humorously when he said that, having been raised on a grim creed of Calvinistic predestination, it came to him as a great relief to find that God was at least as good as some of the elders in his church. Some liberals even worried over the term "Kingdom of God," which seemed to them to imply outworn feudalistic concepts. They suggested that we use a new term, "Democracy of God." They did not indicate whether God was to be the constitutional monarch or the elected president of this democracy. But it would be unfair to suggest that many liberals went to these extremes. Liberals did, however, insist that God owed certain things to man; man could demand certain inalienable rights even from God.

If God is found in the world process, it follows that we are not absolutely dependent upon special acts of revelation. Since one of the liberal's proofs of God is religious experience, and since such experience is not limited to

Christianity, it is clear that other religions also have revelations. Man at his best is, in fact, a continuous revelation of God. Even those who do not recognize God may, in their devotion to high goals, be revelations of God's nature and will. There are differences among liberals at this point. Some, such as D. M. Edwards, would make all knowledge revelation so that scientific knowledge is as much revelation as any doctrine of Christianity. Other liberals are more cautious and believe that God can be found more clearly in Jesus and the Bible than he can be found in knowledge generally. All liberals agree, however, that revelation must be tested by reason and experience. Otherwise, they insist, how can we decide among the conflicting claims of revelation? Surely we are not to be left at the mercy of every fanatic who claims that he has a revelation from God. Many liberals would agree with J. S. Bixler that if some creeds reveal more about God than others, it is only because their prophets and wise men have made better use than others of the sense and wits that God gave them.

With this view of revelation in mind, it is not surprising to find that the liberal welcomed higher criticism of the Bible. Not only did the liberal believe that the Bible has no claim to preferential treatment among the books of man, but the liberal was happy to be freed from the need to apologize for the whole Bible as the infallible word of God. It was no longer necessary to defend a God who ordered the Israelites to kill their enemies to the last woman and child or who sent bears to eat children who poked fun at a prophet.

When the Bible is studied by higher criticism, the liberal

believes that it becomes evident that God has revealed himself through an evolutionary process, just as he created the world. Beginning with primitive, bloodthirsty ideas, the Bible traces how the Jews slowly came to grasp the idea of a righteous God who can be served only by one who does justly, loves mercy, and walks humbly with his God. This progressive revelation of God finds its fulfillment in Jesus, where God is portrayed as the loving Father of all men.

The exact place of Jesus in liberal thought varies with the thinker. There are many liberals who look upon Jesus as divine and as a revelation of God. There are others who find in Jesus nothing more than one of the great leaders of religious and ethical thought. At no point is it more difficult to sum up liberalism in general. William Adams Brown, who for many years was a leading liberal spokesman, is perhaps typical. He argues that Jesus has been an authority for Christians in three ways. First, Jesus is the clearest illustration of the life which Christians desire to live and which they desire to see prevail in society. Jesus is an authority because he enables us to see more clearly than anyone else what the world would be like if everyone were loving. Second, Jesus exemplifies to his disciples the kind of spirit that must prevail if the life of love is ever to be realized in fact. We see through him that without the spirit of self-sacrifice, the good society can never be achieved. Lastly, Jesus symbolizes to his followers the resources on which they must rely if they are to overcome the obstacles which impede the life of love. Man needs aid from beyond himself. In Jesus we see one who was flooded by an inrush of divine love and who found that God was able to supply his every need. Thus he has become to his followers the symbol of what God is like and the channel whereby the love of God may find access to the spirits of men. This statement, while perhaps typical of the center of liberalism, would be criticized by some liberals as too radical and by others as too conservative.

Most liberals were keenly interested in the search for the historical Jesus. They felt that Christianity must be grounded upon the exact type of person that Jesus was. With this went a belief that a careful task of scholarship was needed to restore the true Jesus to view. This search for Jesus used varying slogans; sometimes it said, "Not Christ, but Jesus," signifying that "Christ" stood for a doctrine while "Jesus" represented the simple Galilean prophet. Another slogan was "The religion of Jesus, not the theology of Paul." Many liberals saw Paul as the chief culprit in hiding Jesus behind a smoke screen of theology.

There was far from complete agreement as to what kind of a man the real or historical Jesus was. But, in general, it was felt that he had been the teacher of a simple ethical religion, summed up primarily in the Fatherhood of God and the brotherhood of man. We saw this theme earlier in Harnack, and it is still alive.

The fundamentalists cried in alarm that the liberals were losing Jesus, the center of Christianity, and that the basic doctrine of his divinity was gone. The liberals answered that they were rediscovering Jesus. All that the fundamentalists had was the Christ of the "cradle, cross, and tomb." That is, liberals charged, the fundamentalist was only interested in the fact that the Son of God was born miraculously, that he died a substitutionary death, and that he rose from the grave. But the liberal wanted to bring the whole of Jesus' life once more before the gaze of Christians. The liberal charged that the fundamentalist was so concerned with theological doctrines about Jesus that he forgot to follow Jesus' teachings.

In general, it can be said that as the liberal tends to erase the line between knowledge and revelation, so he tends to erase the line between all men in general and Jesus in particular. All men are potentially the sons of God; Jesus is supreme and unique only in that he fulfilled the potentialities of all men more completely than any other. Those liberals who find meaning in the divinity of Jesus usually insist that it must no longer be interpreted in terms of the Nicene Creed, which says that Jesus was of the same substance as God; rather it must be interpreted in terms of character and spiritual unity. Jesus was one with God in that he completely lived the will of God in all things.

Liberals, as a whole, have usually denied the doctrine of original sin. This does not mean that liberals have been unaware of the fact that man is less than perfect; but the liberals have insisted that there is nothing radically wrong with human nature as such. There is no sharp cleavage between God and man, for man at his best is like God. Man can be won from sin by education and by holding before him the ideals of Jesus. Furthermore, there are degrees of sinfulness; a man can make progress in overcoming sin, and even if he does not reach perfection he can move in that direction.

Many unfair things have been written in recent years about the liberal's failure to understand the sinful depths of man's nature. True, there have been and still are liberals who can say with J. S. Bixler that sin is a theme for the esoteric poet and the disillusioned theologian who reaches into the past to find props for his outworn creed. Bixler also insists that there is an element of artificiality and make-believe in the use of the term "sin"; it is a concept into which we have to argue ourselves. But Bixler is not typical of liberalism.

Many liberals insisted that they were, in reality, taking sin more seriously than the fundamentalist. The fundamentalist, the liberal charges, condemns sin in general but neglects particular sins. The liberal insists that he has less to say about sin in general because he is concerned with the concrete sins such as corrupt politics, selfish exploitation, self-righteous dogmatism, racial discrimination, and so on. Walter Rauschenbusch pointed out, many years ago, that if you have a doctrine of the original fall of man it is a state of depravity so horrible that one is quite likely to pay scant attention to the contributions to sin which have been made by our more recent forefathers or by ourselves.

For all liberals ethics take a central place. At times liberals fall back upon a pragmatic proof of their religion. The truth of religion is to be judged by whether it makes the world a more ideal place in which to live.

This helps to explain the tendency of many liberals to disparage theology. Time, they feel, is wasted in theological debate that could be spent more profitably in ethical activity. Too much theology has no apparent ethical implications or consequences. The acid test of religion is not what a man believes but "Inasmuch as ye have done it unto one of the least of these . . ." For many liberals the philosophy or psychology of religion has taken the place of theology. E. S. Brightman, for example, heartily denied that he was a theologian; he said he was a philosopher with a particular interest in the philosophy of religion. As he saw it, there was no realm for theology that could not be handled by philosophy. This is an almost inevitable conclusion if revelation is either denied or identified with knowledge in general.

An important element of liberalism was the Social Gospel school. The exact relation of the Social Gospel to liberalism in general is difficult to analyze. On the one hand, it was the product of liberalism and most of its exponents were liberal theologians. On the other hand, it criticized liberalism for becoming identified with one class in society, the middle class, and it was from the Social Gospel concern that the radical criticism of liberalism was to come in men like Reinhold Niebuhr. Despite the ambiguity, there can be no question that the Social Gospel was an element within liberalism.

In one sense, the Social Gospel is as old as Christianity. Although from time to time there have been Christians who fled from society and felt no need to make it Christian, the norm of Christian conduct has been to try to Christianize society. Medieval Catholicism certainly had a gospel for society and tried to build a Christian culture. Calvinism had a definite program for society, and it is no accident that all countries influenced strongly by Calvinism became democratic. The Reformation sects all looked in various ways toward the establishment of a Christian social order.

Nevertheless, there was a modern twist to the Social Gospel as it appeared among liberal Christians of the late nineteenth and early twentieth centuries. These men were in reaction against the individualistic gospel that had been presented by the more orthodox and fundamentalist groups. Social Gospel advocates insisted that it is not enough to preach a gospel that is simply fire insurance to save a man from Hell. There is no use saving individuals one by one when a corrupt social system is damning them by the thousands. The Social Gospel sees that man lives in a society and, to a great degree, is molded by his society. If the society is corrupt it will inevitably corrupt man. Quite frequently, the hope for a better earthly society replaced all active interest in a life after death.

The Social Gospel became convinced that by the "Kingdom of God" Jesus had meant neither an afterlife nor a society upon earth which was to be set up by the supernatural act of God in the Second Coming of Christ. Rather, Jesus meant that society in which men are brothers, living in cooperation, love, and justice together. This ideal society is one that man himself, with the help of God, can build. In fact, man has already made many steps in this direction, such as the building of political democracy. At this point the Social Gospel joined hands with the secular faith in progress which was so strong in the first thirty years of this century. This did not mean that Social Gospelers were swept away with the naïve concept of an inevitable progress or that they thought it was a simple and easy task to build the perfect society. Rauschenbusch, who died in 1919, was one of the greatest exponents of this position, and he was well aware that there is a kingdom of evil, that is, a socially organized movement of evil. He saw that social progress can be retarded and lost. Although he threw himself wholeheartedly into the struggle of labor for a more fair and equitable income, he also looked forward to the time when labor, grown powerful, might have to be resisted in the name of the Kingdom.

Social Gospel thinkers did not have any one program for saving society. But they did tend to agree that there are fairly clear choices for the Christian to make in the economic, political, and social realms. Many of them identified the Christian social order with such things as democracy, socialism, the New Deal, or the cooperative movement.

Two problems in particular were close to the hearts of the Social Gospel thinkers—peace and race relations. Many repudiated all future wars, feeling that the First World War had proved their complete futility. Although others could not accept absolute pacifism, there was general agreement that war had to be abolished before the Kingdom of God could appear. The League of Nations won their wholehearted support. It was this school of thought also which saw, long before it came to the view of the general public, that racial discrimination is a blot upon our claim to be Christian.

This, in brief outline, is the essence of the liberal movement, particularly as it appeared during the first thirty years of this century. This summary is not completely fair as a description of any particular liberal thinker, for, as is apparent, independence of thought was very dear to all liberals and such independence does not make it possible to describe all the variations of liberalism in the compass of one chapter. But if it is not adequate to describe any one thinker, it is, I believe, adequate to describe the mood and trends that were winning a victory over fundamentalism and gaining control of the leading seminaries and the official organs of leading denominations from 1900 to 1930.

When liberalism found that it had defeated fundamentalism in the sense which we pointed out in the last chapter, the liberals found that they were sharply divided among themselves. One can detect some four main trends in liberalism, although there are many individuals who cannot be fitted into any one of the four.

First, on the left wing of the liberals there grew up a group known as humanists. In 1933 this group published a manifesto which was clearly naturalistic in philosophy. That is, it denies the existence of God, immortality, and the supernatural in general. For these it substitutes faith in man and his capabilities. Instead of looking beyond himself for help or dreaming of a life after death, man is to fulfill and develop his personality. This leads to the necessity of remaking society so that it will minister to the growth of man. All things are to be judged by the effect they have on man and his welfare.

The humanists claimed to be carrying the ideals of liberalism to their logical conclusions. Liberals had made God immanent; now humanism made him completely immanent: God is the world; God is man and his dreams. Liberals had appealed to religious experience; now humanists identify religion with experience. Wherever there is the experience of the integration of personality, there is religion. Liberals had emphasized ethics and judged religion by its ethical fruits; now religion is to be identified with ethics.

Liberals had humanized the Bible; humanists see that it is a purely human book. Liberals emphasized the humanity of Jesus; humanists see him as a good man, a good teacher, although hampered by a pre-scientific view of the universe. But he is not to be preferred to other ethical teachers past and present. Liberalism, the humanist charged, had recognized the right of science to enter all fields, but somehow got cold feet when it was suggested that science could solve all problems. Liberalism, in short, is condemned for being a halfway reform; its supporters have seen the promised land from afar but have been afraid to enter it.

A second group of liberals emerged under the general heading of "The Empirical Philosophy of Religion." These men sought a religion that could be based squarely upon the scientific method. A. N. Wieman, a leader of one branch of this school, asserts that liberal theology wanted to be empirical but it allowed religious experience into its thought and this opened the door to unempirical subjectivity. Wieman wishes to have a God-centered instead of a man-centered theology. Thus he asserts that instead of looking within to our inner experience, we must look outside ourselves for the reality of God. He asserts that the time has come to quit arguing about the existence of God; God is to be defined so that his existence cannot be denied. Wieman has made several definitions of God, one of which is "God is that character of events to which man must adjust himself in order to attain the highest good and avoid the greatest evils."

Wieman does not believe that we can know about God except by experiment; we must live experimentally to find what values are supported by the universe. For Wieman,

God is a part of nature, that part upon which we depend for the production and preservation of human values. At first sight it may be asked, What is the difference between Wieman and the humanists, since both are naturalists in their philosophy? The difference is that Wieman is trying to find a source outside man which is the basis and background for man's values. The humanist, on the other hand, believes that values are the concern and product of man alone. Nature, apart from man, is indifferent to value.

Another wing of the empirical school has been that which is associated with Personalist philosophy and has found one of its leading exponents in E. S. Brightman. For Brightman, religion is to be based empirically on experience, but experience consists of all conscious life. To test the truth of religion one must test it by its coherence with all other knowledge and experience as a whole. While the philosopher of religion will consider experience that comes from mysticism, revelation, or other sources, each must finally be judged by reason.

Whereas Wieman's God is not personal, Brightman's is. Brightman comes to this conclusion by weighing various facts of experience and finding that the hypothesis of a personal God is the most coherent hypothesis to explain such facts. God is not a person, but is personal in the sense that he includes a rational will and is the source of human values. He is also personal in the sense that human beings may have a personal relationship to him.

The most unique aspect of Brightman's theory is that God is limited. Faced with the problem of evil, Brightman assumes that a completely good and a completely powerful

God would not allow evil. Since he has evidence for believing God to be good, it follows that God cannot be all-powerful. The limiting element is within God himself, as an uncreated given aspect of his nature. Man is thus called to be a co-worker with God in the struggle against evil.

A third group of liberals appeared after the victory over fundamentalism. As an example of their thought we may point to Leroy Waterman's recent book *The Religion of Jesus.*

Waterman finds two religions in the Old Testament, so sharply distinguished from each other that they cannot possibly be interpreted as variations of one faith. First, there is the popular religion of the Jews which is nationalistic, believing that the Jews are a chosen people. The hope of this religion is for the day when God, acting through his Messiah, will set up the supremacy of the Jews over the world. Over against this is the prophetic religion preached by the great prophets but repudiated by the Jews. This religion renounces all nationalism or chosen-people concepts and proclaims that God is for all men. It condemns religious ritual as useless and puts ethical living in its place. It has no doctrine of original sin or of an afterlife, but looks instead for a society of brotherly love on earth.

The prophets were repudiated by the Jews, although their books were kept in the Bible. Their religion would have been lost except that Jesus of Nazareth taught it again, broadening it out with greater emphasis upon the love, mercy, and universality of God. The whole of religion for Jesus was to love God and your neighbor. He made no claims that he was anything more than another prophet. But the Christians, including those who wrote the New Testament, no more understood Jesus than the Jews understood their prophets. It has taken all the skill of modern higher criticism to rescue the gems of wisdom that Jesus taught from the layers of misunderstanding which were poured over them by his followers, beginning with Paul.

In view of the fact that Jesus had to wait two thousand years before anybody understood what he was talking about, it would seem that he died in vain. Waterman faces this question and concedes that the heed given to the religion of Jesus has thus far been negligible. But he feels that there is still time. The world is now threatened with destruction, but if the churches are prepared to make a 50 per cent claim upon the heritage of prophetic religion the present world can be turned upside down and saved. If the churches will make a 100 per cent claim on this religion, we can hope that in a reasonably short time we will transform this world into something approaching the Kingdom of God on earth or, as Waterman prefers to call it, the "Kingdom of *MAN*." Communistic materialism, with a ridiculous philosophy, has swept across half the human race in fifty years and is threatening the whole world. How much more likely that the rational but hopeful faith of Jesus could sweep even greater areas in less time if only it were liberated from the entanglements of theology and church life.

The fourth group of liberals included the majority of the liberal churchmen. Each of the three former positions represents a radical break away from orthodox Christianity. The biblical God has disappeared completely from the humanists and he is hardly to be recognized in the concept of God used by the others. The uniqueness of Christianity is completely lost in all of them, and revelation is mostly denied or ignored. The idea of the divinity of Jesus is either abandoned or given a completely new meaning. The fourth type of liberalism disagreed with the first three on each score.

We may call the fourth type of liberalism "Evangelical Liberalism" in the sense that it retained the essential "evangel" or gospel of Christianity. It is found in men like Harry Emerson Fosdick, W. A. Brown, Rufus Jones, and H. S. Coffin. These men were dedicated to reason, an open mind, and the currents of modernity, but they also were rooted firmly in the Bible and Christian tradition. They were certain of the reality of God, and while they preached his immanence they believed that he transcended the natural world. They found uniqueness in Jesus and the Christian religion and, if they could not go all the way with orthodox creeds, they could stand with the orthodox in accepting Jesus as Lord of their lives.

Rufus Jones was typical of this school. He was deeply interested in mysticism, by which he meant man's direct knowledge of God. God can be known by man as a spiritual power which is available to him. God is the resource beyond man from which man can draw strength. Man is thus a creature who lives in two environments, one earthly and one spiritual. The man who lives in the earthly environment alone, or at least who tries to do so, is not a full man; he is throttling his truest potentialities. The process of salvation is not away from normality but rather the attainment of completely normal spiritual health.

Jones's mysticism led to action. As Fosdick points out,

Jones lived, rather than talked about, Christian conduct. He was, more than any other, responsible for founding the Friends Service Committee, whose works of relief and rehabilitation are of renown across the world.

For Jones the Bible was not an infallible book; there was a real human element in it and, as in all things human, there were error, triviality, and actual evil. But despite this, he asserted that there is a uniqueness about it. Through all of its human weakness, Jones could hear the Spirit of God speaking through the writers, speaking a word to his heart where God also spoke.

Jones feels that the arguments over whether Jesus was divine or human rest upon a mistaken conception of man. If man is completely alien to God, then it is difficult to see how Jesus could be both God and man. But if we believe that man is essentially related to God, created in his image, the problem becomes simple. In Jesus we find one in whom the divine possibilities of man have come to full growth. Because in Jesus a man gave himself completely to God, he becomes the one in whom we can see God. God, being a spirit, could not reveal himself in any complete way except through a person. It takes a person, dedicated totally to God, to show man what God is like. Christ is thus the great center of history; we do not know of what the universe is capable until we see what man becomes in Jesus. The greatest fact of history is that God broke into it through this unique person. But Jones is sure that if God broke into history here, it does not mean that he is absent from history at other times. God reveals that he is present in the whole of history and in the heart of every man.

In the position of this fourth group we find an attempt to keep the God of Jesus Christ and to keep Jesus as the revelation of God. It believes that Christianity can be enriched from many quarters, that all truth belongs to it. But it is not prepared to sacrifice Christianity to the acids of modernity. This represents the meaning of liberalism to most liberals through the twenties and the thirties of this century. Yet it was a position that found itself under great stress, and it is not surprising that as liberalism rethought its position it was from this group that the reorganization came.

CHAPTER 5

The Remaking of Liberalism

One of the most significant events of the last twenty years in theology is that liberalism, in the very moment of its triumph over fundamentalism, began to disintegrate. As early as 1934, Walter M. Horton, a liberal, could write, "Liberalism as a system of theology has collapsed." Horton went on to point out that even liberals hardly ever spoke or wrote without making some gibe at liberalism.

Horton, in pronouncing the demise of liberalism, insisted that there were values in it which must be maintained and preserved for the future, but, to do so, liberalism had to be remade. Ironically, liberalism's "abiding experiences" had to be put into new categories so that a new age could understand them. Liberalism had performed so well the task of fitting itself to the modern age that when the age passed, a new generation came onto the scene for whom liberalism was as difficult to comprehend as fundamentalism had been to its fathers. But, in attacking liberalism, its modern critics overlook one significant fact: liberalism was able to change itself. Liberalism rethought and is rethinking its position. No system that can change itself, as liberalism is doing, can be ignored as bankrupt. A new group has arisen whose members are sometimes called, with whimsy, "repentant liberals." I prefer the term "neo-liberals." Neo-liberalism is the attempt to preserve the values of liberalism while reinterpreting them for a new age and new conditions.

First, we must understand the reasons for the decline of liberalism. Liberals found themselves, in the early thirties, between the humanists and the fundamentalists. It was disturbing to the liberals to find that the criticism from both quarters was strangely similar. Both opponents insisted that the logic of liberalism ought to lead it to humanism. Humanists charged the liberals with "cold feet": they were afraid to trust man and put their hope in human progress as their logic demanded. Fundamentalists had always insisted that this was the logical conclusion of liberalism. William Jennings Bryan had charged that liberalism was simply an anesthetic to put man to sleep while his belief in God was amputated.

During the calm, prosperous days of the twenties, the humanist argument had a tantalizing appeal. Man was rapidly solving the problems of the ages. Science, education, and man's organizational genius were doing what traditional religion had failed to do. Truly it seemed that all we needed was a little more faith in man and a little more effort. But in 1929 this faith crashed with the stock market. America began to learn what Europe already knew, that the twentieth century was not the dawn of Utopia. Faced with the proposition that their presuppositions led logically to humanism, liberals, instead of going humanist, reexamined their presuppositions.

More important in the decline of liberalism than the criticism either of humanist or of fundamentalist were the events of the century. The twentieth century opened as the century of promise, the century in which science, harnessed to the needs of man, was to banish all ills from the face of the earth. In fourteen years it brought the most bloody war known to man. America, isolated from that war, could still keep its optimism in the belief that it had been a war to end wars. Europe could not be so hopeful, and somewhere between 1914 and 1918 liberalism died in Europe. America at first could not understand the strange theology of Barth and Brunner that was born across the Atlantic, but after the depression of 1929 it commenced to search its own soul.

The depression had a deep influence upon America. The great industrial giant sprawled helplessly, unable to overcome the ridiculous problem of having produced too much. President Hoover kept promising prosperity around the corner, but it did not come. Roosevelt and his New Deal gave a spark of hope, but unemployment was not overcome until the threat of another war sent men to work again. In the meantime the totalitarian states had arisen. At first Russian Communism could appear as one manifestation of the coming age of promise. But, by the middle of the thirties, it was seen as a reign of terror to all except those whose need of faith was so great that they had to believe that someone was triumphing over the problems that faced all nations. Then came World War Two, the murder of six million Jews, atomic bombs, the cold war, Korea, and the ever present threat of World War Three. It is not strange that a theology born in the late nineteenth and early twentieth centuries would find that a change in its thinking was necessary.

The central character in Howard Spring's novel *Fame Is the Spur*, looking at the world of 1940 and thinking back over his long life, comments that the world of 1940 is drastically different from that in which he grew up. In the world of his youth "No good had seemed impossible," but now there was an age in which "No evil, no bestiality, no treason or treachery seemed incredible." Modern man began to feel lost. The word "anxiety" became a cornerstone of pyschological thinking. Man sought to get the world back to normal, but those who knew history could only tell him that it was back to normal. The abnormal ages were those idyllic years when "no good had seemed impossible." What could the liberalism of the early twentieth century say to this modern man?

Liberals began to ask themselves some serious questions. If it is obvious to any rational man that the great need of our world is brotherly living, why do not men live as brothers? Liberals like Waterman are right in saying that the great need of our time is that men should follow the teaching of Jesus and the prophets. We ought to love our neighbors as ourselves, and thus put an end to war, economic injustice, racial discrimination, and other evils that now threaten to destroy man or make his life a nightmare. But have these liberals realistically faced the implications of their reading of history? Why is it that man has refused so consistently to follow the simple, rational way to salvation? It will not do to say that man has not been properly taught, for all cultures have emphasized these ideals. Can it be, liberals were forced to ask, that there is some truth in orthodoxy? Is man inherently sinful? Is there a radical weakness in man's nature which turns him from the self-evident way of his own salvation?

Recently a burglar was caught rifling a safe while a burglar alarm clanged madly outside the door. His captors asked him why he had not fled when he heard the alarm. His answer was that he was hard of hearing. Is this, asks the liberal, a parable of man's situation? With the alarm clearly ringing all about him, man goes on his self-destructive way. Can it be that man has a flaw in his character as fatal as the burglar's faulty hearing?

In the light of these questions, neo-liberals were forced to doubt that the real problem is to tell man how he ought to live. On the whole, man seems to know that. Is not the real problem how to remake man so that he can do what he ought? Was Paul perhaps presenting the true human situation when he said, "But how to perform that which is good I find not" (Rom. 7:18)? If this is the case, do we not need something more than a teacher of ethics in Jesus? Do we not need a savior who can release us from the bondage to sin? The neo-liberals do not have any one set of answers to these questions, but they have all agonized over them.

The threat to liberalism did not come simply from the events of the time; there was also a reappraisal of many of the facts and theories upon which liberalism had built. For one thing, the idealistic philosophy went out of fashion. I say "went out of fashion" because, as W. M. Urban points out, it was never disproved. New philosophies became fashionable, in America a positivistic naturalism, and in Europe a radical existentialism, neither of which was friendly to liberalism.

The Bible became a problem for liberals. For one thing, if the truth of the Bible is only that which we can experience in more modern categories, and which we can know by reason, why bother with the Bible at all? Why spend all the trouble in searching for the historical Jesus when he says nothing but love God and your neighbor, things which we can figure out for ourselves? Is there a hidden element of authoritarianism in the liberals who have renounced authoritarianism? Does a truth of reason gain more cogency when we find it in the Bible or spoken by Jesus? Why do we spend more time dissecting the Bible than the *Analects* of Confucius if there is nothing unique about the Christian faith?

This question became more pointed as the direction of biblical scholarship in the twentieth century became clear. We cannot say that archaeology and biblical criticism have proved the truth of orthodoxy, but in recent years they have given more comfort to the orthodox than to the liberal.

We can mention a few ways in which this is so. The liberal interpretation of the Old Testament was firmly grounded on the theory of Wellhausen, a nineteenth century German scholar. This theory assumed that, by dating the writings of the Bible, we could reconstruct the history of how its ideas developed. In the light of this an evolution was found in the Bible from its early primitive beginnings in polytheism, up through stages to belief in one ethical God. This view was presented to the lay reader in Fosdick's well known book *A Guide to Understanding the Bible*. But the trend of the times is indicated by the fact that a leading Swiss biblical scholar calls Fosdick's book "an obituary of last century's scholarship." It is now seen that Wellhausen was, to a large extent, rewriting history to fit Hegelian philosophy with its concept of evolutionary development. Archaeology makes it seem probable that Israel's monotheism goes back at least to Moses, a point completely denied by Wellhausen.

Archaeology has helped orthodoxy in two other ways. It has strengthened belief in the reliability of the Old Testament as history. Secondly, its newly discovered knowledge of biblical times points up the uniqueness of the biblical religion. Seen against the world of its time, biblical faith shines like a lonely diamond on a sandy beach.

Liberalism, however, has been disturbed most by the developments of biblical scholarship in the New Testament field. The nineteenth century scholarship was analytic; it took the Bible to pieces and analyzed the parts. The result was a seeming conglomeration which lacked unity and enabled the liberal to set one part of the Bible against another, for example, Paul against Jesus. Twentieth century scholarship, using the results of analysis, has gone on to synthesis, and it has become increasingly clear that the Bible in general and the New Testament in particular represent a unity.

The quest for the Jesus of history has turned out to be a will-of-the-wisp. We have learned much from the efforts. Jesus stands forth much more clearly in all of his manhood, his beauty of character, and his moral power. But he is not the Galilean carpenter who taught a simple ethic for whom the liberals were hopefully searching. Instead, modern scholarship finds a man who was conscious of a heavenly destiny and who announced himself as God's chosen agent for the salvation of men. Paul's gospel about Jesus is not radically different from Jesus' gospel about himself.

As a consequence, Paul is no longer the villain in scholarly circles. He cannot be honestly portrayed as the perverter of the simple gospel that Jesus taught. The basis of Paul's gospel and the gospel of the earliest Church is now known to be identical. Paul is no longer seen as a Greek thinker who brought in concepts from the mystery religions; his background was Jewish and Christian.

Furthermore, John's Gospel, a stronghold of orthodoxy, can no longer be banished to the outer darkness of neglect by critical scholars. Recently discovered fragments of the Gospel prove that it was being circulated at the end of the first century, which is earlier than many scholars formerly thought that it was written. Scholars are no longer so dogmatically certain that it was not written by the disciple of Jesus. At certain points it is recognized as better history than the Synoptics.

A. M. Hunter summarizes the findings of New Testament scholarship in this century with this significant passage:

"Despite the aberrations and excesses of individual critics, the course of New Testament studies in the twentieth century has been mainly to make more sure the foundations on which our Christian faith is built, and to increase and deepen our conviction that a 'new face' has been put upon life by the blessed thing that God did when he offered up his only begotten Son." [1]

In short, archaeology and biblical criticism in the last fifty years have been far from supporting liberalism at its most

[1] A. M. Hunter, *Interpreting the New Testament, 1900-1950* (Philadelphia, The Westminster Press, 1951), p. 140.

crucial points. When liberals, at the turn of the century, threw in their lot with the biblical critics, and swore to follow wheresoever truth led, they hardly bargained that they would be led back to orthodoxy. Of course, the liberal can still cling to the few "individual critics" that Hunter mentions, but such a process is distasteful. The liberal cannot forget that he despised the fundamentalist in the earlier controversy for quoting a few scholars who had lost contact with the main development of critical thought.

Such, in brief outline, are some of the reasons why liberalism has fallen into difficulty in our generation. But if liberalism is true to its central method, if it is truly trying to mediate Christianity to the world in which it lives, and if it is ready to follow reason and experience, it ought to have the ability to adapt itself despite the blows that have fallen upon it. This is precisely what the neo-liberals are trying to do.

The most decisive moment in the changing course of liberalism occurred one Sunday morning in 1935 when Harry Emerson Fosdick stood up to preach in his beautiful skyscraper church in New York. This man was the great symbol of liberalism. Reinhold Niebuhr has pointed out that he was that rare combination, a great preacher and a great theologian. For many years his voice brought the message of moderate liberalism over a nationwide radio hookup. His books were best sellers. Although Fosdick was never one of the most radical liberals, the fundamentalists quite rightly singled him out as their most dangerous enemy. Here was a man who had the ear of millions and who, in persuasive and beautiful language, was reasoning men into liberal Christianity. Humanists likewise saw in Fosdick the chief antagonist, the leader of liberals who refused to "follow their logic" to humanism.

Although ordained a Baptist, Fosdick was called to the First Presbyterian Church of New York. Presbyterian conservatives carried on a battle to have him replaced and finally passed a statement of faith which all non-Presbyterian ministers in Presbyterian congregations had to sign. Fosdick refused and went to the Park Avenue Baptist Church on the condition that it would be a creedless church, accepting all into membership who desired to enter. His congregation later built the present Riverside Church, one of the leading Protestant churches in the nation.

On the before-mentioned Sunday, in the midst of the depression, Fosdick dropped an unexpected depth charge into the sea of theology. His topic was "The Church Must Go Beyond Modernism." It was by no means the first storm warning to arise in liberalism, but when Fosdick, the unofficial general of the liberal army, spoke out, the change in liberalism became apparent. The fundamentalists shouted in glee and many a liberal felt betrayed by his leader. Neither attitude was justified. Fosdick had not ordered a retreat; he had laid the plans for a new attack.

Fosdick began that memorable sermon by insisting that the church had had to go modernist; he was not backing down. He told how a boy, fifty years earlier, had cried himself to sleep in terror lest he go to Hell, while his mother, out of patience with the religious teachings that had caused the fear, tried to comfort him. "That boy," said Fosdick, "is preaching to you this morning." Modernism was essential, claimed Fosdick, if men were not to have their intellect in the nineteenth century and their religion in the sixteenth.

But, necessary though modernism was, it was not enough. It aimed, quite rightly, to make religion speak to the times, but it had to do more than accommodate itself to the times or it would be shallow and transient. Fosdick found in particular four weaknesses in modernism.

In the first place, modernism had been excessively preoccupied with intellectualism. Its great goal had been to adjust Christian thinking so that a modern intellect could understand and accept it. Necessary as this was, it is no more than one of many problems. The deepest experiences of man's soul, whether in religion or elsewhere, are not just matters of the intellect. We are wise to use our heads; but rather than to approach problems head first we should do better to approach them heart first, conscience first, imagination first. Man is greater than his rational process, and to be preoccupied with the intellectual problem is to handle only a portion of man's life. Furthermore, the critical spiritual problems are no longer intellectual; they are moral. Can Christ meet the problem of sin in our personal and social lives? What our modern world needs is not so much souls intellectually adjusted to it as souls "morally maladjusted to it."

In the second place, modernism has been dangerously sentimental. This is due to the fact that the late nineteenth and early twentieth centuries to which modernism adjusted itself were buoyed up by the illusion of inevitable progress. Thus modernism had eliminated the idea of the moral judgment of God. Granted that the former horrors of theology had to be rejected, it was sentimentality, not realism, that supposed there was nothing to fear in God. Sin, personal and social, is real, insists Fosdick, just as our forefathers told us, and we can see that, as they told us, sin leads men and nations to damnation.

In the third place, modernism has watered down the concept of God; it has adjusted itself to a man-centered culture. God was relegated to an advisory capacity as a "kind of chairman of the board of sponsors of our highly successful human enterprise." It is necessary, said Fosdick, to turn again to theology, the problem of existence, the problem of what is eternally real. If the materialist is right and this world is nothing but matter and man is just the accidental result of the fact that the cooling off of the earth produced the necessary conditions for him, then it is ridiculous to find dignity or glory in him. The time has come to quit being apologetic; we must quit acting as if the highest compliment that could be paid to Almighty God is to have a few scientists believe in him. Christianity has its own standing ground, the only one that can give hope to man: it proclaims that the eternally real is spiritual, that the highest in us comes from the deepest in the universe.

Finally, Fosdick charged, modernism has too commonly lost its ethical standing ground and its ability to launch a moral attack. It has become too well harmonized with the modern world. It is all very well to accommodate one's thought to astronomy and biology, but when one gets into the habit of accommodating and begins to adapt oneself to nationalism, imperialism, contemporary capitalism, and racialism, then it is dangerous.

Fosdick closed with a challenge. Modernism has won the battle it set out to win; the fundamentalists are now in the backwaters and the future of the Churches is with modernism if it will have it so. Therefore, let the modernist battle cry be, not "Accommodate yourself to the prevailing culture," but "Stand out from it and challenge it." We cannot harmonize Christ with modern culture, for Christ is a challenge to it.

I have summarized Fosdick's sermon at considerable length because it represents the basic tendencies in the neo-liberal movement. I speak of tendencies because the group has not formulated any detailed position which is held by all members.

As we suggested earlier, Fosdick's sermon, with its symbolic significance, had been preceded by many storm warnings. Young liberals like Walter Marshall Horton, John C. Bennett, and H. P. Van Dusen were warning that liberalism had to change its ways if it was to speak to the modern man. Many of these younger liberals banded together under the slogan of "realism." The name, however, is too vague and is applied to thinkers of widely different views. The term "neo-liberalism" serves better to indicate the organic relationship to liberalism that characterizes these thinkers even in their reaction to its early twentieth century forms. As Horton said, "Liberalisms perish, but liberalism remains."

The term "realism" implies that these liberals have abandoned idealistic philosophy. They are looking outside man, not within, for the clue to God. The subjective experiences of man are put second to man's knowledge of a reality apart from himself. God is no longer thought of in terms of a construct of man's mind, but as a factor in man's environment to which he must adjust himself.

In line with this, the neo-liberals have criticized the liberals for constructing God in terms of what they would like him to be, instead of searching for what God really is. Liberals had argued against attributing certain characteristics to God because they seemed immoral or, in short, because they did not fit into what the liberals wanted God to be. But, says the neo-liberal, we must adjust ourselves to what God is whether we like it or not. Instead of preaching only those doctrines that promise to be pragmatically useful to man in building a better world, we must preach those which are true.

Part of the realism of neo-liberals is their firm resolve to face all of the darkest and worst facts about the human situation. Elton Trueblood gives to one of his books a title that expresses their concern—*The Predicament of Modern Man.* Central to all neo-liberalism is the realization that man is in a predicament, that life is no simple success story, that the predicament calls for something more than fine-sounding ethical ideals. In a world like ours, as Herbert Wallace Schneider says, man "does not need to seek God, but finds himself driven to God."

Horton is forced to realize that God approaches man, as it were, with two hands. The one hand is open to woo us with love, but the other is a mailed fist which will crush our best laid schemes if they do not accord with his will. God longs to have us accept his loving approach, but when we do not we find that we are crushed with depression, war, psychological maladjustments, and the destruction of our civilization. The gulf between the two hands can only be bridged by Christ and his Church. Yet there is hope even in the mailed fist of God, for it assures us that every evil system bears the seeds of its own destruction.

The realistic analysis of the predicament of man drives neo-liberalism to the realization that the orthodox doctrine of sin is, in many ways, more realistic than the liberal optimism about man. Shortly after the turn of the century, G. K. Chesterton, a Roman Catholic layman, chided the liberals that they had dropped the only doctrine of Christianity which could be empirically verified, the doctrine of original sin. Neo-liberals have come to see the point. Without restoring the full Augustinian position, neo-liberals have recognized real truths in it.

The position of most neo-liberals would not be too different from that of John C. Bennett as he outlines it in his chapter of a book called *Liberal Theology*, edited by D. E. Roberts and H. P. Van Dusen. Bennett wishes to keep certain truths of liberalism. First, it recognized that man is essentially good as the creation of God. All men, not simply Adam before the fall, are created in the image of God. Man, as we find him, is not essentially evil but is "as a good thing spoiled." Augustine realized this, although some of his followers have forgotten it. Second, we must realize that man is also a finite child of nature, subject to the laws of nature. In light of this, Bennett cannot follow those orthodox thinkers who have supposed that man's impulses, such as sex, are basically evil. Man dies because he is an animal, not because he is a sinner. Third, man is a rational being, and rational living in the widest context is good living. Reason is our protection against false revelations. Fourth, man is free and responsible for his actions. Fifth, man can find his true self only in social relations. Loyal membership in communities is the major content of the good life.

But Bennett also accepts truths from the Augustinian tradition. First, there is the doctrine of sin. Sin cannot be defined simply as those choices which are made in the knowledge that they are sinful or opposed to the will of God. The real human problem is that we so easily deceive ourselves and thus persuade ourselves that our evil acts are really good. Second, we have to learn from Augustinianism that there is sin on every level of moral and spiritual growth. Every human good can be corrupted. In short, a perfect life is not humanly obtainable. Third, because of the foregoing, all Utopian hopes are illusory. The perfect social order cannot be built upon earth. This does not mean that there can be no changes for the better, but it does mean that progress will never be free from the danger of serious setbacks, and every reform will have its unexpected by-products of evil. We cannot assume that our achievements will lead to the Kingdom of God on earth. Fourth, we are led to recognize that repentance is a continuous necessity. Such repentance keeps us from self-righteousness and contempt for others in their sinfulness.

It is evident that neo-liberalism is unable to be as hopeful for solving man's dilemmas as was liberalism. It is not so sure that a particular social activity can be called Christian. Social Gospel liberals always knew that the present American capitalist system cannot be called Christian. Neo-liberals are willing to concede that it could not be replaced by a perfectly

Christian system. This does not rob the neo-liberal of hope. He can still work for improvements in any social situation, but he is not led to expect unqualified success.

Likewise, the neo-liberal is increasingly convinced that society and man cannot be remade simply by education and science. The drag of self-centeredness in human nature is such that mere educational manipulation or scientific improvement cannot overcome it. Social reform must always make use of means of coercion as well as of persuasion. Religion must offer a power to change man's life as well as education in ethical ideals.

Inasmuch as God is no longer identified with man at his best, neo-liberals are ready to admit a need for some kind of mediator between God and man. Since we cannot find God by looking at man, God must reveal himself. Once more neo-liberals are turning to "Christ," not just the "Jesus of history." They have not come to any agreement upon what is meant by the divinity of Jesus, but they are increasingly aware that it must be taken seriously. Jesus is not just the best that man has accomplished; he is a gift of God to man. Georgia Harkness probably speaks for her fellow neo-liberals when she asserts that in this area we need convictions without dogmatism.

One of the significant aspects of neo-liberalism is its new sense of the importance of the Church. Since Fosdick called them to stand over against the world and not simply conform to it, neo-liberals have felt the need of a place to stand. Added to this has been the experience that the leaders of the movement have had in the ecumenical movement where they have seen the Protestant Church organizing itself and trying to understand itself.

Liberals in general had little concept of the Church. To many liberals the Churches were simply social organizations of men gathered together because of a common religious and ethical concern. The necessity of the Church was purely practical: men are able to do more when organized than as individuals alone. It is typical of liberalism to be prophetically critical of the Churches as they exist. Liberals criticized both the division of the Churches and their failure to live the teachings of Jesus.

Neo-liberals are dissatisfied with this liberal concept. They have not ceased to express the liberal critique of the condition of the Churches, but they have come to believe that there is a Church over and beyond the split denominations. It is a living society, begun in the work of Jesus and continuing that work through the ages. It is not just another social organization to be explained in sociological terms; it is a divine institution, founded by God. Walter M. Horton even goes so far as to say that as Christ had a divine and a human nature, so has the Church. Not all neo-liberals would go that far.

Neo-liberals have not found complete agreement upon any set of beliefs. They are still on the march, searching for a camping ground. They are one only in their belief that there are values in the liberal method and approach which must be preserved but which to be preserved must transcend the forms in which liberalism spoke twenty years ago. For most of them, this means a rediscovery of some of the beliefs of orthodoxy which were surrendered by liberals. The fear of slipping back into fundamentalism over which liberals triumphed so recently has kept many of them from accepting more of orthodoxy than they might otherwise have done.

George Hammar, a Swedish theologian who made a survey of American theology about thirteen years ago, came to the conclusion that neo-liberalism was a highly unstable form. It was a transition theology, he believed, which had not yet been able to break completely from its liberal moorings nor to throw in its lot with a true orthodoxy. Thirteen years later it does not appear that the transitional nature of neo-liberalism has been overcome. Whether it will be a transition to a new liberalism or to a complete break with liberalism we cannot yet say. One thing, however, is certain. There have grown up powerful theological movements which have broken completely with liberalism. In fact, neo-liberalism is, in large part, a response to these movements, and to them we now turn our attention.

CHAPTER 6

Neo-Orthodoxy: The Rediscovery of Orthodoxy

It would seem that man had lost his ability to invent new titles for his systems of thought and instead is tacking the prefix "neo" onto old titles. We hear of neo-Darwinianism, neo-Freudianism, neo-Malthusianism, and so on. We have already encountered neo-liberalism in theology. It was perhaps inevitable that there should arise a "neo-orthodoxy."

Nevertheless, the term "neo-orthodoxy" seems particularly inappropriate. "Neo" implies the new and different; "orthodoxy" implies the old and traditional. One is reminded of an event in Canadian politics. The Canadian Conservative party went out of power in the early thirties and has not been able to return. A few years ago its leadership came to feel that its name was a stumblingblock in a land that was forward-looking and progressive, so it changed its name to "Progressive Conservative." A political opponent, writing a satirical essay on the change of name, entitled his article "The Progressive Conservatives: or How to Go Forward Backwards." Neo-orthodoxy seems to have the same implications. It is only fair, therefore, to point out that the name was not coined by the representatives of the movement but by their opponents.

Despite its paradoxical flavor, the term is a good description. The essence of the movement has been a return to orthodoxy, but it is orthodoxy with a difference. It is a position which is held usually by former liberals and it is deeply colored by the fact that its representatives were liberals. This coloring may be discerned in two ways. On the one hand, certain aspects of liberal thought are found in the new movement. Fundamentalism is repudiated as savagely by the neo-orthodox as it is by the liberal. Biblical criticism is accepted in its most radical forms. But the fact that the neo-orthodox are converted liberals is also found in the extreme reaction against certain liberal concepts, such as the use of reason or natural theology.

We must take time to define some terms. Ever since Thomas Aquinas there has been a distinction between natural and revealed theology. Natural theology means man's philosophical study of religious questions. Natural theology is all that man can learn about God, immortality, and such questions, by the use of reason alone. It appeals to facts and theories that are available to any rational man. It is distinguished from revealed theology, which begins with the belief that God has given a special revelation of himself. Thus Aquinas believed that we can prove by natural theology that God exists, but it requires revealed theology to inform us that there is a Trinity. It can be summed up quickly by saying that natural theology represents man's search for God; revealed theology represents God's search for man.

In light of this distinction, it is clear that the liberal method, with its emphasis upon reason and experience, made much of natural theology, going so far in its philosophy of religion as to make it the only theology. Neo-liberalism represents a trend to give revealed theology a new hearing without abandoning natural theology. Neo-orthodoxy repudiates natural theology almost completely.

One of the founding fathers of twentieth century neo-orthodoxy is the nineteenth century Danish philosopher-theologian Sören Kierkegaard (1813–1855). In the nineteenth century Kierkegaard was a voice crying in the wilderness of a complacent civilization. His cry went unheeded except for the self-satisfaction which newspaper editors got from plaguing him. But in the anxiety, loneliness, and despair of this century the words of Kierkegaard began to ring as true prophecies. The experience that he found unique in the nineteenth century has become common in the twentieth. He seems more up to date than any philosopher our century has produced. From him we get the philosophy known as "existentialism," which for some time has been popular in Europe. Ironically, he has given atheists and Christians about equal inspiration.

The facts of Kierkegaard's tragic life are well known and we will not recount them here. There are many popular works upon his thought, and we will mention only a few of the more important aspects of his thinking.

Kierkegaard was an existential thinker. That is, he insisted that true thought must begin with the fact of a concrete man in a concrete situation. Abstract truths about man might be true of all men in general, but they would describe no man in particular. Whereas Descartes started his philosophy withdrawn from life, alone and engaged in pure reasoning, Kierkegaard begins with man as he exists in relation to God, the universe, and other men.

Kierkegaard revolted against abstract thought in philosophy and religion. In science or mathematics we can deal objectively with facts without ourselves being deeply concerned with them. But in philosophy and religion the aim is never to know dogmas or ideas but to live them. He protests against those philosophers who build magnificent houses of theory but who do not choose to dwell in them. The aim of true religious or philosophical thinking is to bring man to commit himself to a way of life. If thought does not help man to answer the question, "What ought I to do?" it is a betrayal of man.

We particularly need the existential method, thinks Kierkegaard, when we deal with God or man. In objective thought we think coldly and rationally of objects separate from ourselves. We are not vitally concerned with them in our whole being. They concern our mind or reason only. But it degrades both God and man to make them into objects of this nature. God can never be just an object of man's thought; he is the living challenge who forces man to make a decision. God is subject and not object when he comes into contact with man. Similarly, when we think of others or ourselves as objects, we dehumanize man. We must see man as a subject, the center of a willing, thinking, hoping, passionate process. Man is a self, not a thing.

With this goes an emphasis upon man as an individual. Kierkegaard foresaw what has become so demonic in our day: the tendency to submerge the individual into the mass, to make him simply another cog in the wheel of society. Man can cease to be truly human by allowing himself to be swallowed by the crowd. Existentialism fights to preserve man as the one who makes his own decisions in concrete situations. Kierkegaard deplored the fact that people in the Christian Churches were stereotyped into Church members instead of being free, independent individuals who were answerable to God.

Turning to his interpretation of Christianity, we find that Kierkegaard poses a new question. Both the fundamentalists and the liberals have been preoccupied with the content of religious faith. The fundamentalists believe that we have a set of divine truths which are proved by the authority of Scripture. Liberalism believes that in Christianity we find the highest expression of those truths which man knows dimly everywhere. Kierkegaard opposes both by asking, not what is the content of Christianity, but what does it mean to be a Christian? How does one become a Christian? Of course, the differences are relative, but it is interesting to recall Fosdick's charge that liberalism was overly concerned with the intellectual problems of Christianity.

The problem was made urgent for Kierkegaard because he felt that the members of the state Church in Denmark were not Christian; they were only nominal Christians. Being a nominal Christian actually prevented one from becoming a true Christian. Furthermore, for Kierkegaard this became the question of how one becomes truly human. Just as membership in the Church does not make a man truly Christian, so being born a man does not make one truly human. In essence, Kierkegaard answers that we are not saved; that is, we do not become Christian and human by coming to know something that we did not know before; rather we are saved by the transformation of our existence and life through divine grace. The Gospel is not a new philosophy; it is the act of God which comes to solve the problem of man's despair. Kierkegaard is convinced that one does not become a Christian; he simply strives to become one. He may start on the path but he will not reach the goal.

Kierkegaard believed that one could only become a Christian by a leap of faith, a radical commitment of one's whole life. That is because man's reason comes up against a boundary beyond which it cannot penetrate. The reason which can prove things in science is incapable of using the same methods to understand God, for God can never be just an object whose existence can be proved or disproved. When God is known he appears paradoxical to our reason. The God that men claim to find in their philosophies is but an image of themselves. The real God can be found only in so far as he makes himself known as a living factor in life.

But the leap is not irrational even if reason cannot prove its desirability. When man studies his true situation he is driven to despair, and in his despair he is ready to grasp the salvation that God offers to him. Man sees that he is bound by the finite world but he is pulled toward the infinite. His dreams exceed his grasp. He longs for the good life but fails to live it. So long as man eats, drinks, and is merry he may hide from himself the underlying anxiety and insecurity of life. But the minute he takes seriously the ethical life, he is brought to despair by his failure.

Doubt is never completely overcome; but in the leap of faith whereby he chooses to follow Christ, man has the moral certainty of his conviction. With Kierkegaard, modern theology finds a new understanding of religious certainty. Kierkegaard promises no certainty; he offers instead a leap which is always, in part, a leap in the dark and a gamble that there is a God. Faith means the betting of one's life upon the God in Jesus Christ.

Faith does not mean for Kierkegaard the believing of doctrines that cannot be proved; it means the giving or commitment of one's whole life. There is no halfway house; one either accepts or rejects Christ. Those Christians who try to hide in the Church as respectable persons are seeking a halfway house, but they are greater enemies of Christ than the atheist. He had particular scorn for preachers who made a good living out of preaching about the crucifixion of Christ. For Kierkegaard, to become a Christian one had to give his whole life to the dangerous and lonely task of following God. It was dangerous and lonely because it had always to be lived against the crowd and often against the Church. The Christian life is a life of suffering; there is no simple peace of mind in Christianity for Kierkegaard.

Kierkegaard's God is always transcendent. This is not a philosophical doctrine to be set against the liberal's doctrine of immanence. Instead, it means that man is separated from God by his sin and guilt. Man cannot lift himself to God; God must come to man. Even in the leap of faith to God, God must act. Although Kierkegaard repudiated predestination, he was aware that without the help of God we cannot find God.

This, in too brief an analysis, is something of what Kierkegaard has to say. He has greatly influenced modern theology. Karl Barth and Emil Brunner, at whom we are about to look, were influenced deeply, even if they react against him at certain points.

KARL BARTH

In 1919 the peaceful atmosphere of European theology was thrown into confusion by a commentary on the book of Romans written by an unknown minister, Karl Barth. One writer says that Barth took a letter, written in koine Greek during the first century, and made it read like a special delivery to the twentieth. A new word came into the theological vocabulary: Barthianism. It is impossible to ignore this movement, which has spread over the whole Christian world. Every modern theologian owes something to Barth, even if he has only reacted against him. The forcefulness and vigor of Barth's writing is such that there is no room for neutrality.

Barth was a leading figure in the German Church until Hitler's rise to power. When Barth refused to take the loyalty oath to the new regime he had to flee to Switzerland, where he has remained. He has been active in the ecumenical movement, often sounding a strong minority position. His theology is difficult to describe because it has been undergoing continual change and development, although its basic principles have remained firm. It is also difficult to describe because Barth has been a voluminous writer. In addition to a host of pamphlets and books he has written the *Church Dogmatics*, a monumental work of nearly six thousand pages, although it is still incomplete. Barth often complains, with justice, that his critics are attacking ideas that he does not hold. This, he believes, is the result of their failure to read his *Dogmatics*. None the less, we ought to have sympathy with the critic who has not mastered the six thousand pages, most of which are not yet translated and none of which is light reading.

Barth began his career as a liberal theologian with a hope that the Kingdom of God would soon be achieved through the building of a socialist society. The First World War came as a shock to his optimism. As he watched the civilized nations plunge themselves into the orgy of destruction, he felt that man's problem was too desperate to be solved by merely changing the economic structure. For a time he was bewildered. In particular, he was overcome by the demand of his weekly sermon. People, he reflected, came to hear him each week, but what could he say? Too often they went away disappointed because the sermon was not answering the questions that troubled them most. To such persons, he could not simply preach his own opinions or any man-made philosophy. They wanted something more than a commentary upon current events.

In due time he came to feel that the only thing to preach was the Word of God, which could not be identified with the preacher's words. The preacher must preach so that the Word of God could make its own witness to the congregation. The preacher might prepare the way, but it was God alone who could speak his Word to man. It was from this starting point that what Barth calls his "marginal note" to theology was developed.

Barth believes that this is a day of crisis. Judgment has gone forth upon the Western World, which has ignored the distance between God and man. He is certain that Christianity can be saved only after it has disassociated itself from the dying culture. But the crisis of our day is the symptom of the eternal crisis that arises whenever man is confronted by the living God. Man, in his daily life, meets situations in which he must make decisions, but the decisions are never simply between man and man. God is always present speaking his Word. When God confronts man there is a crisis, for man has to make a choice; he must accept or reject God's way. To accept God requires a humility that modern man seldom achieves.

Barth charges that the liberal theologian is wrong on two counts. First, the liberal starts with himself; that is, he builds his world view upward from man. He uses reason, natural theology, and mystical experience to build a system in which God can be found. But, says Barth, the only God that can be found by such a method is a pale reflection of ourselves. The second error of the liberal is his optimism. He forgets that he is a "dying man speaking to dying men." Instead of this man-centered faith we need to come to the crisis in which we recognize our helplessness. When we see this we will be ready to wait for God to speak to us. Hence preaching must no longer appeal to the strength of men, challenging them to do things; rather it must force men to face their weakness until they turn to God.

In Barth's theology there are always two worlds, time and eternity, sharply distinguished because God is "Wholly Other" and cannot be known by an analogy with anything that we possess or are. The relation of God to man, therefore, cannot be expressed in neatly logical forms. It can only be expressed in paradoxical statements such as, "Jesus was both God and man," or, "In revelation God is both revealed and hidden." This aspect of Barth has been widely misunderstood. It is often argued that if God is Wholly Other he cannot be known even in revelation, for man cannot understand God's Word unless there is something which God and man have in common. A closer analysis of Barth's meaning proves that this and similar objections do not apply.

When Barth says that God is "Wholly Other," he is not denying that there is some analogy or similarity between God and man. He is trying to establish God as an objective reality. Against those who apply the term God to the "spirit of humanity" or to the "value-producing aspects of the universe," Barth wishes to insist that God is a reality existing independently of man and the world. Furthermore, Barth wishes to deny that we can come to know the nature of God by starting with man at his best and adding a few superlatives. God is not simply the culmination of all that is good in man. When man has done his best, he must still look to God for forgiveness, for God's way is higher than man's achievements.

When Barth insists upon the two worlds of time and eternity he is attacking the liberal concept of immanence. This is not a denial that God is at work in the world nor does it imply that the affairs of the world are of no concern to God. Barth refuses to sanction any division of life into the sacred and secular. He does not deny that we live and move and have our being in God.

The gulf which Barth finds between God and man, time and eternity, is the gulf dug by man's sin. Because of sin, man's knowledge or power cannot take him to God; God must come to man, for God always has the initiative. Man's search for God never finds God; it finds an idol. It is only because of

God's search for man that men may have communion with God. Barth is anxious to emphasize that man can never have any kind of control over God; God cannot be an object of our knowledge. He is eternally the subject who is known only when and where he chooses to speak. God has spoken, not in nature or history, but only in Jesus Christ. In Christ God came down and took the form of man to speak so that man could comprehend his message. Man can understand God, the Wholly Other, because God has graciously chosen to make himself like unto us. The gulf between God and man, time and eternity, has been bridged by God.

Through their religions, including the Christian religion, men are trying to find God. But inasmuch as man's search for God is doomed to failure, religions become veils which prevent men from seeing God. Jesus comes as the revelation that destroys religion, including the Christian religion. The early Christians were called atheists because they destroyed the man-made gods of their time, and it would be a healthy sign if Christians were still suspected of atheism. Christians have also created gods in their lives instead of listening to the true God.

Because God is the living God, Barth warns against identifying the Word of God with the words of the Bible. He believes that the error of fundamentalism is its attempt to read the Bible as a "self-sufficient Paper-Pope." The words of the Bible and the man Jesus are simply tokens. One may read the Bible countless times without hearing the Word of God, just as many saw Jesus without seeing God. But the Word comes to us through these tokens. Some day, as we read a passage of Scripture, it may come alive and speak to us in the situation in which we find ourselves. In the same way the words of a sermon may become tokens which enable God to speak to the listener. Revelation is thus not knowledge about God; it is God himself acting in man.

This means that the Word of God is always spoken to a particular man in a particular time and place. The Christian revelation is not like a proposition of logic which is unchangeably true to all persons in all times and places.

The gulf between God and man is formed by man's sin. Sin has corrupted man's relations with his fellow men and with God. Because of sin God cannot be found in history because history is the story of man's defiance of God. Neither can God be found in nature, for sin blinds man's eyes so that he does not recognize the work of God. In fact, sin is such that we recognize its full power only after we have been delivered from it. It is one of Barth's paradoxes that sin can only be overcome when we confess our sin, but we cannot confess our sin until it is overcome. At this point Barth finds himself expressing a form of predestination.

For all of his emphasis upon sin, Barth has warned us that we must never make sin more important than grace. Sin has already been overcome and defeated by Christ. The Christian does not need to fear sin; he can celebrate a victory over it. Yet it seems fair to say that for Barth the victory over sin is primarily the victory of God's forgiveness. Barth has little to say about new moral strength which enables the Christian to live without sin.

Barth, as we have seen, denies natural theology and extols faith over reason. In one place he says, "Faith takes reason by the throat and strangles the brute." As a result, Barth is charged with being an irrationalist and an obscurantist. Before we decide whether or not this is true, we must understand what Barth is denying when he denies reason. He is not denying that we must think rationally about our Christian faith. This is illustrated by his discussion of the Trinity, wherein he points out that the doctrine is not revealed as such in the Bible, but that when men rationally analyze the implications of revelation they are forced to Trinitarian thinking.

What Barth is saying in his denial of reason is twofold. In the first place, he denies that man's reason is free from sin, as many liberal and Catholic writers seem to think. He denies that man's reason remains pure and objective, unsullied by the selfishness that expresses itself in his other activities. A man can become as possessive and selfish over "my truth" as he can over his houses and barns. Reason is no cure for our problems because it can be used for good and evil alike. Because selfishness uses reason, it follows that the God which man finds by reason is the God he wants to find; that is, it is an idol. Reason must be purified and cleansed before we can think rightly about God.

The second objection to reason arises from the nature of revelation. The knowledge of God is not something that we can know by a priori thought. God reveals himself in concrete situations as an "I" to a "Thou." That is, God is not a general principle of truth; he is a personal will who meets man in man's existential situation, or, as we might say, God meets man where man actually is. When God reveals himself, it is not as the Supreme Being of philosophy or as some general truth; it is as a demand or claim that forces a man to decide upon a course of action. Because of the personal nature of God, he remains free in revelation. Man does not possess the knowledge of God as an inalienable right; it is a gift which God gives when and where he chooses.

Barth agrees with Kierkegaard that reason cannot defend the Christian revelation. Either Jesus was or was not what he claimed to be—the unique Son of God. The man who tries to prove Christianity has never really believed. He is more dangerous than the man who tries to disprove it. The man who would prove it implies, implicitly or explicitly, that he has some criterion higher than revelation by which he can judge claims to revelation. But if a man has a criterion higher than revelation, he does not need revelation. On the other hand, if he does need revelation, it must judge him; he cannot judge it. The Word of God must be its own proof, for there is nothing higher by which it could be proved. As a result, Jesus comes to every man with the challenge, "Follow me," and thereby sets up a crisis in the heart of man. Either a man follows or he does not. He must choose, and his choice is a leap of faith.

Barth's teaching about the relation of Christianity to society has undergone great changes. He began, as we saw, with the optimistic faith that a Christian socialism could save the world. After the World War destroyed this hope, he became extremely pessimistic. In his Commentary on Romans he argues that the man who would reform society is so tainted with sin that he can do no more than replace one unjust system by another unjust one. Christianity must reconcile itself to preaching its gospel in an alien and unchristian world. Even when Hitler came to power Barth announced that he was going to carry on his theological work "as if nothing had happened." As time passed, however, it became evident to Barth that the new regime was so opposed to the will of God that it had to be defied. He called to his fellow Christians to take to the catacombs rather than to accept it. This led Barth to exile. Since that time he has recognized that while the perfect social regime cannot be built, the nature of the political society does make a difference to the Christian's Church and life.

Barth believes that Christianity must never be identified with any particular political or social system. Man's social trouble stems from the fact that he does not limit his demands upon life. As long as man demands all he can get and more, there will be rivalry among men for the things of the world, which will, in turn, lead to exploitation and class struggle whether the society be capitalist or socialist. The Church can and must take a stand upon urgent social problems, but in doing so it must not suppose that it has a final or absolute solution. It must continue to point to God, who stands in judgment over all of man's achievements.

Behind Barth's thinking on social questions, as behind all of his thinking, is his eschatological viewpoint. Eschatology deals with the "last things," the final culmination of life and history. Here too the distinction between time and eternity is decisive for Barth. This time, in which we live, is moving to its end; it must be taken up into eternity. This is the significance of the Christian faith in the resurrection of the body; it is faith that our present existence will be changed by God into a new relationship in which it will be fulfilled and completed. This is the Christian hope.

Barth speaks often of the end of the world and of the Second Coming of Christ. The end of the world is not the stopping point or boundary of life so much as it is the goal to which we are going, the harbor toward which the ship of life is sailing. The Second Coming does not mean the same to Barth as it does to the fundamentalist. It is not to be separated from the Resurrection of Christ. In the Resurrection Christ was made supreme over the world, the conqueror of sin, evil, and death. But the victory of Christ remains a hidden victory, seen by the eyes of faith but hidden from the eyes of the world. The Second Coming represents that point where the victory of Christ will be made manifest to all eyes, and the world will know what the Church already knows—that Christ is Lord. Barth has been careful not to try to picture what the Second Coming will be like or when it may occur.

This explains further why Barth is sure that Christianity cannot be identified with any political movement or achievement. Such an identification would be to try to achieve the Kingdom of God within time. But the Kingdom can only come when time ends and eternity rules.

The Christian is forced to live in the world, and he cannot escape it. We are not yet in the Kingdom of God. The order of the world can be preserved, even in its best forms, only through the use of force and coercion. No state can exist without using force or threatening to do so. Furthermore, the order maintained by the state is never simply justice; it also includes injustice, strife, and bondage. All of this is opposed to the love of God. The state is necessary, for without it there would be worse injustice and strife. But service to the state is dangerous for Christians; it is implicit disloyalty to God. The fact that we cannot escape this dangerous and ambiguous situation is evidence that this world is the world of sinful men. Our reconciliation with God has been accomplished by Christ's death, but it remains a hidden fact in this sinful world. In such a situation our only hope is that Jesus Christ, risen from the dead, promises the coming age in which our reconciliation will no longer be hidden and the evils of time will be transcended in eternity.

This brief summary will make it clear that Barth has had to fight his theological battle upon two fronts. He has been attacked by liberals because his rejection of philosophy and reason as means to know God seems to lead to obscurantism. His renewal of orthodox doctrines such as original sin, the supremacy and uniqueness of Christian revelation, and even predestination seems to some to place him among the fundamentalists. None the less, he has been attacked by the fundamentalists who are shocked at his denial of verbal inspiration. In fact, Barth is willing to accept the most radical criticism of the Bible inasmuch as he does not believe that the Word of God is to be identified with the words of the Bible. Because of this position, Barth's greatest service has been to act as a gadfly to his theological generation. In the light of his thought others have been forced to rethink and reevaluate their positions.

EMIL BRUNNER

When the term "neo-orthodoxy" is used, two names usually come to mind, Karl Barth and Emil Brunner. Brunner is a native of Switzerland and for many years was a professor of theology at the University of Zurich. During the early part of his career he was known as the leading disciple of Barth, but in the thirties Brunner and Barth found themselves in sharp disagreement on certain issues. In 1953 Brunner moved and inspired the Christian world by giving up the security and prestige of his professorship at Zurich to go to Japan, where he is now teaching in a Christian college.

The break from Barth came when Brunner published an article criticizing Barth. The issues involved were those of natural theology. Brunner denied that the image of God in which man was created had been completely lost through sin, as Barth said. He believed that there was some revelation outside the Bible. He also charged that Barth leaves no room for the new nature of the redeemed man to grow out of the old nature. Barth answered this with a counterattack in his pamphlet "Nein."

Despite his defense of natural theology, Brunner is no friend of liberalism. He denies that we can build a system that will start from natural theology and will include revealed theology. Man does have a natural knowledge of God, but it is always blurred and distorted by the sinfulness of man and thus it cannot save him. The relation of Barth and Brunner at this point may be put this way. Both agree with the Reformation concept of the primacy of Scripture. Barth interprets this to mean that the Bible is the only source of knowledge about God. Brunner interprets it to mean that the Bible is the only criterion by which we can judge the truth or adequacy of the knowledge of God that arises elsewhere. This difference has many practical implications. To the man outside Christianity, Barth has to present the Christian faith on a "take it or leave it" basis, because there is nothing in the man's thought which can form a common ground for discussion. In a real sense Barth cannot even debate with philosophy because he preaches that of which philosophy is completely ignorant. Brunner, however, can recognize truth in the philosopher, atheist, or adherent of a non-Christian religion and thereby enter into a meaningful debate with him. Brunner will insist that ultimately the other man has neither sufficient nor completely true knowledge of God. Nevertheless, he will concede that the other has a partial truth, and from this common ground a discussion can begin and persuasion may be possible.

Brunner accepts the Augustinian analysis of original sin, but repudiates Augustine's theory that it is inherited. The essence of sin, feels Brunner, requires a free decision; the Christian doctrine is opposed to the concepts of fate that one finds in Greek drama. Original sin is a result of man's choice, not his heredity. Man is created by God for a life to be lived in harmony with God, but instead he lives a life centered around himself. Man withdraws into his "I" castle and can only be brought out when God comes to him with love and, winning his confidence, overcomes his anxiety and enables him to give himself away.

Brunner has done much to spread the concept of the "I-thou" relation with God, a concept that was originated by Martin Buber, the Jewish thinker. This concept is meant to analyze the nature of our knowledge of God. The knowledge of God is to be contrasted sharply from what Brunner calls "objective" knowledge. In objective knowledge that which is known is an object outside oneself. The purpose of such knowledge is to get power over that which is known and to learn how to manipulate it. In objective knowledge the knower is always cool and detached; he has no vital concern with the object. There is no communion between the knower and known. There is a cleavage between the subject and the object that he knows. The primary example of objective knowledge is science, where the knower stands outside his experiment, controlling and manipulating it but detached from it.

Subjective knowledge has often been set over against objective. For Brunner this is a false antithesis. The true alternative is not subjective knowledge but the personal relationship which he calls "I-thou." It is one of the tragedies of life that not all of our relations with other people are "I-thou" relations. We live in a world where all too often the other becomes for us just another object in a world of objects, to be known for the sake of controlling and manipulating him. The peril of the social sciences is that, in trying to be scientific, they copy the natural sciences; but this leads them to treat people as things, things to be manipulated and controlled, or reconditioned, molded and brainwashed. But occasionally our relations with another cease to be impersonal; the other ceases to be an "it" or a "something" and becomes a "thou." He reveals to us, not some information about him, but himself. He gives something of himself and we give of ourselves in return. An "I-thou" relation has replaced the objective relationship in which we were as two things facing each other. There is now communion. No longer is one an onlooker who may be enlarged by more information. Instead, he is changed to the very core of his being because he knows and gives himself to the other.

This personal relation is the best analogy to our knowledge of God. It is a mistake to suppose that we can have an objective knowledge of God because this would imply that God comes into our power and is held, controlled, and manipulated by us. This, believes Brunner, is the mistake of Roman Catholicism and fundamentalism. Each believes that it has, in its system, infallible truths about God which it can use to judge others and to win salvation for itself. But God is truly known only in an "I-thou" relation. It is the essence of the "I-thou" relation that we never possess, control, or manipulate the other. In this experience we approach each other and commune in freedom, giving of ourselves freely. The same principle applies to the "I-thou" relation with God; we cannot possess or hold God in our creed, Bible, or Church. God remains free. Revelation does not give some knowledge about God; it is God giving himself. God must give himself because only God can reveal God.

This explains why natural theology or philosophy can never have an adequate knowledge of God. In philosophy we are thinking about God; God is an "it," an object whose existence or non-existence can be debated. When a philosophy class discusses the proofs of God, it may have a most pleasant time; it may even learn something about the use of logic. But it can learn nothing about the God whom Christians worship, for the word "God" means something entirely different in the two spheres. This is proved, among other things, by the fact that no great difference in the lives of two men is noticeable, although one has accepted the proofs for this "God's" existence and the other has rejected them. But the God of Christian revelation cannot be so blithely discussed, accepted, or rejected. To know this God is to be shaken to the depths of one's being and to be remade.

The term "I-thou" and the fact that an analogy is drawn between it and the "I-thou" relation of individual men and women must not be interpreted to mean that God and man meet as equals. Quite the contrary: God is known always as the Lord of one's life, as the One who has the right to command full obedience. But the sting of obedience is withdrawn by the fact that in obeying him we find our true selves, the selves that we were created to be.

Because the "I-thou" relation is a personal relation, it must be free. Brunner refutes any form of predestination or determinism. The concept of predestination is an attempt to solve the problem by a too rational method. It is logical but it fails to do justice to the complexity of the relationship. The truth in predestination is that we know God because he first knew us, that is, because he came to us before we were ready or willing to go to him.

The Bible points to a particular time and place where, in Jesus Christ, God chose to make himself known. Christianity, therefore, remains a "scandal" to the modern mind which desires to find a God who may be known anywhere at any time by anyone who tries hard enough. Behind this modern desire there is a refusal to face the fact of man's sinful preoccupation with himself. We cannot logically deduce how the just God is going to behave toward sinners. It is only because God has actually appeared to reveal his forgiving nature that we are able to speak with assurance of God's forgiveness of sin. Because of man's sin, God can be known only through a mediator, Jesus Christ, who comes from God with the revelation that man could not find for himself.

Brunner is confident that there is no such thing as Christian faith apart from Christian conduct. His book *The Divine Imperative*, a volume of nearly 600 pages, is one of the classic treatments of Christian ethics to be written in this century. He spends the first part of that book in analyzing the theological basis for ethical living and then turns to the application of that analysis to specific spheres such as the state, the economic system, and the family.

Brunner starts with the recognition that every man has some concept of what he believes to be the good life. As a fact of history, he finds that morality has been closely connected with religion and that all religions have a concept of a law which comes from a divine will. Despite this, there has been, since the time of Socrates, an attempt to find a rational ethic which does not depend upon a revelation of God. This attempt may or may not be irreligious, but its religion must be one that is known by man's reason alone.

From the efforts of rationalists we get two basic systems—the naturalistic and the idealistic. The naturalistic systems treat man as a product of nature, an animal, and try to find in nature the clue to good living. Such ethics have to face a dilemma. Man is conscious of a "sense of ought" which often calls him to do what does not come naturally. Either the naturalist must deny the validity of such a consciousness or he must bring a non-naturalistic element into his system.

The idealists, most of whom are influenced by Kant, try to build an ethic upon the basis of duty for duty's sake. Man is aware of the "categorical imperative," the sense of feeling that he ought to do something regardless of inclination or the profit to be gained by the act. But, asks Brunner, what can "Thou shalt" mean if it does not come from God? Who is the legislator that makes it right? Idealism forces us to split the personality so that we think in terms of a better self which legislates to our worser self. In Kant, his own Christian training shines through his thought and colors it continually where he believes that he is using reason alone. But in others this kind of ethic can lead to identifying one's inclination with one's duty.

In his book *Justice and the Social Order*, Brunner analyzes what happens to the concept of justice when it loses its basis in the will of God. The age of rationalism explained the sense of justice in terms of man's reason alone. In the nineteenth century the positivists, denying all supernaturalism, insisted that justice is a purely relative matter, varying from one place to another. They denied that there is any eternally valid concept of justice standing over human legislation. From this it followed inevitably, believes Brunner, that states should grow up which would cast aside all traditional concepts and proclaim that the only standard of justice is the will of the ruling power. In short, you get totalitarianism, in which the state can do no wrong because there is nothing higher than the law of the state by which it could be judged. Hence, if there is no "sacred, eternal, divine, absolute law," it is impossible to denounce any law or national act as unjust. We cannot attack the totalitarian state as a monster of injustice; we can only say, "It does not suit me; I do not like such things."

In Christianity Brunner finds the alternative to naturalistic positivism or subjective idealism. In the Bible goodness has its basis solely in the will of God. It is God who speaks the "Thou shalt." In the face of this command we can understand the full meaning of guilt, but we do so without despair for with the knowledge of guilt comes the assurance that it can be overcome by forgiveness.

In the light of this law we find that all men are sinners; all have fallen short of God's will. It is only through the mercy of God that we can be considered righteous. The worst sin is not, therefore, any of the obvious vices; it is the pride of the man who thinks he is good enough and who looks with scorn upon other men. This man is continually forced to water down the demands of the law in order that he might justify himself and appear more righteous in his own eyes.

In Christianity goodness does not arise from a sense of duty. Obedience is not the fruit of a sense of ought but the free act of love. The self-centered man is lifted out of himself by God's love, which has no conditional "I will love you if . . ." This is the meaning of Christian freedom: man no longer has to obey a law; he freely does that which he has come to want to do. God does not give commands to slaves; he gives instruction to sons.

When love has freed man from law, it creates a new relation between a man and his neighbor. Love replaces the abstract law between them. No longer is the other man a "case" to which the unbending rule must be applied; he can be loved for what he is, and treated upon the basis of his individual need.

Society is organized in certain "orders of creation," such

as the state, the family, and the Church. These are God-given orders, for apart from them there can be no stable community life. But, although they are God-given, they become tainted with sin, and the Christian does not owe unquestioning loyalty to any of them.

The tragedy of original sin becomes most apparent when we find that our calling in these orders forces us to do that which is evil. For example, a Christian judge must enforce laws even when they are unjust. He knows that society must observe law in order to exist, and so, with a heavy heart, he must administer the unjust law. Nevertheless, he is not confined to his official role alone, and it may be possible to mitigate the sting of injustice in some personal relation with the man who has been wronged. Where a system of law is wrong, it is the Christian's duty to work for a better law; but he must not forget that any law which keeps order is the best until a better order can be achieved.

Brunner has lectured several times in America, and owing partly to this and partly to his more positive concept of natural theology and reason he has been more popular in this country than has Barth. European neo-orthodoxy, however, in either Barth or Brunner, is still viewed with considerable suspicion in America. When Americans become neo-orthodox they are likely to prefer their own domestic form. This brings us to Reinhold Niebuhr, leader of the return to orthodoxy in this country.

CHAPTER 7

American Neo-Orthodoxy: Reinhold Niebuhr

There can be no question that Reinhold Niebuhr is the most important living American theologian. This would be admitted by those who disagree with him as well as by those who follow him. There is no theologian who has made such an impact upon the general public as has Niebuhr. His books are read carefully by many who would not normally be "caught dead" reading theology.

Niebuhr, a professor at Union Theological Seminary, has been prominent in an incredible number of activities. He has been a leader in the ecumenical movement of Protestantism. He has run several times for public office upon the Socialist ticket and, more recently, he has been active in the top echelons of the New York Liberal party. Because he was one of the first political liberals to see the true nature and danger of Communism, he became one of the founding fathers of Americans for Democratic Action. There are few Christians who have given so much time and support to the Zionist cause. Somehow he has found time to write a host of books, edit two religious journals, and act upon the editorial staff of secular magazines. His articles have appeared in a countless number of secular and religious publications.

If we are to understand Niebuhr's theology, we must realize that it is not something which was thought up in the quiet of an academic environment. It grew out of his turbulent life and his efforts to apply Christianity to the social, economic, and political spheres. Niebuhr's thinking always begins with the human, the material, and the social. He did not turn to orthodoxy because it was orthodox or because it came with some kind of dogmatic authority. He accepted it because he found in it the most adequate answer to the problems of social living.

Niebuhr graduated from a seminary in 1915 filled with the convictions of liberal theology. He believed in the goodness of God and man, in the desirability of applying the Sermon on the Mount to the whole of life, and in the optimistic hope that the Kingdom of God could be built upon earth in the relatively near future. Had he gone to a suburban middle-class church he might never have become a great theologian. He went, however, to a small working-class church in Detroit, where he saw at firsthand the problems of the worker, the tactics used to suppress union organization, and the tragic cost in human values that America was paying for its rapid industrialization. He began to doubt that the problems of the time could be solved as simply as his theology had led him to believe.

As time passed, the hard facts of life forced Niebuhr to realize that Christian orthodoxy was more realistic and intellectually respectable than liberal theology. In fact, Niebuhr desires that we should see his theology as simply a rediscovery of the lost wisdom of Christian orthodoxy. This does not mean that he turned to fundamentalism. His use of the term "myth" makes this clear.

The relation of man to God, the finite to the infinite, cannot, says Niebuhr, be expressed in purely rational or logical terms. It can only be expressed in myths such as the Genesis story of the creation and the fall. In religion, he believes, we are dealing with the mystery and depth of life which elude our efforts to catch them in neat rational descriptions. Niebuhr compares theology to a painter who, working upon a flat surface, tries to create the illusion of another dimension, depth. This is a deception, but a deception that describes a truth about reality. Similarly, the theologian must describe God and his ways in the thought forms of our space-time world. But God transcends the world so that none of the things we say can be adequate. On the other hand, God does not simply transcend the world; he is also immanent and active within it, so theology can say something about him. Since our earth-born logic can speak, but not adequately, about God, it must, like the painter, use symbols that point to another dimension of reality. Theology is the attempt to express the dimensions of depth in life. Niebuhr applies the term "myth" to this form of thinking. The term is perhaps unfortunate, as "myth" implies a fairy tale to most people. But by myth Niebuhr means that which, although it deceives, none the less points to a truth that cannot be adequately expressed in any other form. It is deceitful and yet true, just as is the deception of depth which is attained by the artist.

Fundamentalism takes the myths literally and thus enters

into conflict with science over evolution. But such an interpretation is not only absurd science, it is also false religion. It oversimplifies the relation of God to the world. Liberalism saw in these myths only simple folk tales and prescientific speculation. Niebuhr, however, insists that we must take such myths seriously but not literally. So interpreted, they reveal true insights into the God-man relationship. For example, the story of Adam and Eve does not describe the first man and woman historically, but it is a mythical statement of the situation of every man and woman.

A serious misunderstanding often arises from the term "neo-orthodoxy." It is usually used to put Barth and Niebuhr indiscriminately into the same school of thought. It is true that Niebuhr has had a greater respect for Barth than many Americans, but there are vast and significant differences. Niebuhr's works contain many criticisms of Barth at crucial points. This difference between Barth and Niebuhr is clear when we look at Niebuhr's view of the place of reason in theology.

Niebuhr finds in the history of Christianity two attitudes toward reason. One has made Christianity completely irrational, over and above reason. It can neither be proved nor disproved by reason; any natural theology must be idolatry and any attempt to prove revelation must be presumptuous. Niebuhr finds both Kierkegaard and Barth here. He feels that this is dangerous because it destroys the meaning of the Gospel. If revelation has nothing to do with what we know by reason, how can we understand it? Furthermore, this way of thought lacks any standard by which we distinguish true from false revelation. Kierkegaard's passionate commitment to God is a healthy antidote to half-hearted faith, but without reason it can say nothing against the Nazi who passionately commits himself to Hitler.

Side by side with the anti-rationalist Christian, there has always been the rationalist Christian, says Niebuhr, from Origen and Aquinas to modern liberalism. This school has believed it impossible for reason and faith to contradict each other. Faith must be rational. The mistake of this school, believes Niebuhr, is that it prematurely grasps some principle of rationality to which all life must conform. It interprets all reality in terms of nature or mind, or in terms of nature and supernature. It knows clearly where reason ends and faith begins. In short, it pretends to know too much. As he puts it, it claims to know "the geography of heaven and hell, and the furniture of one and the temperature of the other." But life comes to us full of mystery and contradictions. We sense that there must be some meaning to the whole, some system; but if we try to find that meaning and system too quickly we fail to do justice to all of the facts. Niebuhr feels that most rational systems are too afraid to admit the paradoxes and contradictions of existence, and consequently they force life into their theories. They deny or ignore aspects of reality in order that they may keep their system coherent and rational. This is particularly true when they try to fit man into their systems, for man remains a paradoxical and contradictory creature. Any simply rational explanation of him must be an oversimplification.

Niebuhr may be said to have applied the Christian virtue of humility to thought. Christian humility does not mean abject servility; it does not mean pretending that one is less than he really is. It means honestly facing oneself and recognizing one's limitations. Niebuhr tries to do this with reason. He does not, with Barth and agnostics in general, insist that reason can know nothing about the ultimate meaning of human life. But neither does he pretend that reason can know all.

Niebuhr lays a new basis for a rational defense of Christianity. In the first place, he insists that we must make a radical distinction between the natural world and the world of human history. The justification for this lies in the unique character of human freedom. Events do not happen in the life of man with the same necessity that rules nature. The social sciences cannot, in the very nature of things, predict events with the accuracy that we find in the physical sciences.

The events of history come to the believer as given; they cannot be anticipated by some rational theory. Among the events of history are those that reveal God. We find an analogy for revelation in our relations with other persons. We have evidence that there is in the other person a depth of reality that is more than just a physical organism. We have evidence that we are dealing with a "thou," not just a thing. We cannot know the other "thou" if we simply observe his behavior, because his real essence remains hidden. This other person can only be understood when he speaks to us and reveals something of the underlying depth of his being. The word which he speaks is at once a verification of the fact that we are dealing with a different dimension than that of physical existence alone, and it is a revelation of the precise character of the person with whom we are dealing.

The same is true of God. We have intimations that this world points beyond itself, that it is not self-explanatory, that there is a depth of reality which does not meet the eye. But we cannot know this other dimension of reality unless it speaks and reveals itself to us. Christianity is based on the faith that God has spoken in the events of the Bible and particularly in the life of Jesus.

This faith in the revelation of God cannot be proved. To take Niebuhr's own illustration a step further, we may point out that neither can we prove that the character which another person reveals to us in his words is truth. In all love and friendship we accept the other's words in trust and faith. Similarly, we must accept the revelation of God with love, trust, and faith. But this does not leave us helpless, as Barth suggests. Niebuhr believes that the insights of revelation can be applied, by reason, to explain and understand the contradictory aspects of reality. Reason cannot of itself prove the truth of revelation, but, given the revelation, reason can show that it gives a more adequate picture of reality than any alternative. Niebuhr thus argues for the acceptance of revelation because he believes that the hypothesis of biblical revelation is the most adequate to explain and redeem human life.

Niebuhr demonstrates this by a twofold method. On the one hand he attacks alternative hypotheses, such as humanism, to show that they fail to do justice to the whole of life; they explain too much away. On the other hand, he interprets the Christian hypothesis to show that it does do justice to the whole of life. The failure of modern philosophies to interpret or comprehend the disturbing facts of the twentieth century has made Christianity relevant. The failure of modern philosophies does not prove Christianity true; we must still walk by faith, but their failure does make it thoroughly reasonable to try Christian faith.

Niebuhr's most characteristic concept is that of original sin. This does not mean that man inherits Adam's guilt; it means that man falls naturally and inevitably into the sin of claiming for himself and his interests more than their objective importance would warrant.

Sin arises from the fact that man is a finite creature, an animal, who is capable of spirituality. That is, he is capable of thought, hopes, dreams, morality, and he is able, so to speak, to stand outside himself and to judge himself. The finite part of man threatens his spiritual nature. The meaning of life is threatened by man's dependence, animal nature, and inevitable death. Man longs for perfect knowledge, perfect freedom, perfect behavior, and perfect justice, but what he attains is always less than these. Because man is spiritual he needs to have a meaning for life, a reason for living. Because he is finite, every meaning that he finds is threatened. This dual nature of man results in anxiety. To overcome his anxiety man tries to grasp some ledge of security which will be safe from the vicissitudes of life. Man may sink into the sensuality of the animal and cease to strive for ideals, but more commonly he asserts himself, in pride, at the expense of others. Man refuses to recognize his limitations, and claims for himself that which belongs to God alone. Man's sin thus arises from the same source as his creativity and nobility. It does not detract from man's dignity to recognize that he is essentially a sinner, for sin is only possible in a creature who, in part, transcends a purely animal existence.

Pride manifests itself in three forms, each of which is an abortive attempt to find security and meaning for life in spite of its anxious insecurities. First, there is the pride of power. Power exalts a man and makes him feel more secure. It enables him to think that he is above the insecurities that plague the common run of mankind. The lust for power leads man to misuse his power over his fellow man through totalitarianism, racial discrimination, imperialism, and so on. Second, there is the pride of knowledge. Man claims to have the whole truth and nothing but the truth. Because any realistic admission of the relativities of his knowledge would threaten the meaning of life, he defends, often fanatically, his system of truth. He covers his anxiety by pretentious claims to a knowledge that he would like to have but never really has. Third, there is moral pride. This is classically portrayed by the Pharisee who uses his goodness and religion as a means to exalt himself over his fellow man. He thanks God he is not as others. This expresses itself in religious intolerance, persecution, and lack of sympathy for "sinners" on the part of the "good" people.

Normally, in the modern world, man expresses his pride by identifying himself with social groups such as nations, classes, Churches, or races. He finds his security by identifying himself with the power, knowledge, or goodness of his group. This is one reason why religion is not necessarily good. Religion is simply the final battleground between God and man's pride. Religion may lead a man toward true humility or it may lead him to thank God that he has seen the light while lesser breeds without the law still move in darkness.

The chief problem of modern man, in Niebuhr's eyes, is his "easy conscience." Pride leads him to claim for himself a perfection that is not his. This self-righteousness blinds him to the justice and truth of those who oppose him. Man rationalizes his actions to make them appear to others and to himself as more just, ethical, and ideal than they really are. Consequently, the worst evils do not arise from pure selfishness; they arise from self-interest cloaking itself in high ideals. Even man's good actions are nullified by pride.

A Negro student once told me that she would not attend meetings of the Race Relations Society because she could not bear being used by its members to prove that they were more righteous in their racial attitudes than others. A member of any minority group will tell you that he prefers the bigots who hate him to the persons who go out of their way to round him up so that they may demonstrate their superior goodness. This illustrates Niebuhr's point that good actions loose their goodness when performed with pride. He finds copious illustration for his analysis in international relations, where the absolute self-righteousness of a nation makes impossible harmonious relations with other equally self-righteous nations.

The only cure for man's sin lies in the Christian doctrine of salvation by grace. Man's sin does not lie in his animal nature or in his bodily desires. It arises from man's attempts to escape anxiety. As long as man believes that he is capable of conquering his anxieties and building his own security, he will be again tripped into pride. He must face realistically his insecurities and realize that they can only be overcome by God. Man's anxiety leads to sin when faith in God does not overcome anxiety. The Reformers were right: the basic sin is not any deed that man performs, but the separation from God which precedes the deed. By faith in God man can overcome his anxieties. This will protect against pride for two reasons. First, man realizes that it is God and not himself upon whom his security rests. Second, man, realizing his imperfection, knows that his relationship with God rests upon God's forgiveness and not upon his own righteousness. He can no longer scorn his "sinful" brethren, for he knows that he is as sinful as they are. Traditionally Protestants have argued that a man could not go to heaven unless he were saved by grace. Niebuhr argues that we cannot solve the major problems of social living without such salvation.

Niebuhr does not believe that even the Christian finds perfect security or freedom from pride. Pride ever waits to catch the Christian in the worst form of sin—the pride of being good. The Christian, however, has found the means whereby his pride may be humbled and to which he can return in repentance.

In the light of this, Niebuhr is critical both of secularists and of theologians who mutually condemn each other and claim that their believers are more righteous than the others. It is as silly for Christians to feel themselves morally superior by reason of their faith as it is for the secularists to regard themselves as superior for their lack of faith. Christians have some sorry blots upon their record, and many truths have come into history through secularism. The Church must learn the truth that secularism has to teach; it must admit that many of the values of our modern culture are due to secular contributions. The Christian believes that his religion contains a more ultimate truth than the philosophy of the secularist, but he cannot claim that because of this he is always more righteous and wise or that he ought to be more powerful. The major heresy for the Church, be it Catholic or Protestant, is for it to identify itself with God, to suppose that opposition to its way is opposition to God's ways. When the Church is guilty of such pretensions, it needs to be, and usually is, attacked by a secular force. The secular voice becomes a judgment of God upon a Church that has forgotten its true nature.

It is widely known that Niebuhr has spent most of his active life in battling for a more Christian social order. Yet many people insist that there is no basis in his theology for such action. His theology should, we are told, drive a man to despair and inaction. This misunderstanding is partly due to a failure to read Niebuhr with care, and partly due, as D. R. Davies suggests, to the failure of many in our day to understand the depths of life.

Niebuhr tells in his classes a story which no doubt had considerable effect upon his thought and which illustrates his position. In his Detroit pastorate, while he still held a liberal theology, he was teaching a Sunday-school class about the Sermon on the Mount. Having expounded eloquently upon turning the other cheek, he was challenged by one of the boys in the class. This boy made a living for his widowed mother and family by selling papers. Each day, he said, there was a fight among the newsboys to see which one would get the best corner upon which to sell papers. Was he, as a Christian, to turn the other cheek, allow another boy to take his corner, and thus reduce the support that he could give to his family? Niebuhr found that his theology had no answer.

This story illustrates Niebuhr's belief that society never faces us with simple moral alternatives. The tragedy of social life is that one must choose the lesser of two evils rather than an abstract absolute good. The man who insists upon following literally a system of moral absolutes will find that he is making an ineffectual attack upon social evils. Because he fails to see the ambiguity of his actions, he will fall into self-righteousness. We must recognize the tragic necessity of doing the best we can in the circumstances even if it is not an undiluted good.

This concept was first developed in the book with the suggestive title *Moral Man and Immoral Society*. In view of Niebuhr's doctrine of sin, it is clear that he did not think that individuals are moral. But he did insist that individual acts can be conducted on a higher moral level than social acts. Social situations are always an ambiguous mixture of good and evil, altruism and egoism. When a man attaches himself to a social group, he does so with mixed motives. He is altruistic in his willingness to sacrifice himself and even die for his society. But egoism lurks in the background; it is "my country" for which he is ready to die. The original sin of pride can express itself through a society more naturally than through an individual. I can claim for my nation, my race or my political party that which would be ridiculous if claimed for myself.

Because of the nature of society, reforms are never made

simply because of a moral appeal. Capitalists did not reform the abuses of the capitalist system because preachers told them to love their neighbors. They reformed, grudgingly, when labor unions gained the power to force concessions. There is always a latent power struggle between nations and between societies within a nation. Justice is not gained by moral appeal but by establishing a tolerable harmony between the conflicting claims of groups.

Herein, insists Niebuhr, lies the Christian basis for democracy. Many theories of democracy are based upon the faith that man is rational and good and so should rule himself. This is an illusion. If man did not have a capacity for justice, democracy would be impossible. But it is man's sinfulness which makes democracy necessary. Democracy is necessary because no man is good enough to be allowed unchecked power over others; the original sin of pride means that man will misuse his power to exploit others if there is no control over him. Niebuhr believes that this was recognized by the writers of the American Constitution when they created the system of checks and balances to protect the people from too much power in any person's hands.

Niebuhr adopted from Barth the interpretation of the Christian ethic as an "impossible possibility." Jesus taught a perfect, and therefore an impossible, ethic, making no concessions to the weakness of man or to the relativities of the social situation. He demanded the absolute: "Resist not evil," "Be ye perfect." Jesus did not teach rules or laws for conduct; he taught an absolute principle—love. The ethic of Jesus is not, as the liberals thought, another expression of the prudential rules of conduct which the common sense of many ages has formed. On the contrary, Jesus teaches a love so perfect, so self-forgetting, that no man can attain it in the life of the world. But it is not an irrelevant ethic. While there is no situation in which the love-ethic can be applied perfectly, there is no situation in which we cannot come closer to fulfillment of the ideal than we have yet done. It stands in judgment over every situation and calls the Christian to lift up his eyes to a still higher goal.

Niebuhr's concept opposes two extremes. Against the general optimism of American life he has insisted upon the impossibilities of the ethic. Those who fail to see the perfection of Jesus' ethic usually end in complacently accepting as "Christian" a life which is nothing more than dull respectability. But against the despair of much European thought Niebuhr points to the possibilities. In every situation there are still untried opportunities to apply the spirit of love.

Niebuhr believes that it is impossible to identify Christianity with any social achievement. The Christian must be an eternal revolutionary. The kingdoms which we build are not the Kingdom for which we pray. Every social reform is ambiguous. It appears more just to those who profit from it than it does to those who do not. Furthermore, any advance made remains under the peril of later corruption and loss. One reformer can usually see the defects in another man's plans for reform, but the Christian, says Niebuhr, is the man who can see the defects in his own plan.

To Niebuhr, the great mistake of liberalism has been its belief that man is essentially good. Believing that man has sufficient resources in himself to obey the teaching of Jesus, it follows the Kantian principle, "If I ought, I can." Therefore, liberals have believed that the defects of society can be removed by changing the social system and by education. These theories founder on the rock of man's sin. Sin does not result from the imperfections of society; it causes them. When the old exploiters are removed, new exploiters appear.

This gives rise to a dilemma. If man faces realistically the limited possibilities of his achievements, how can he work for a better society? It is obvious that most reforms in the past have been brought in by men who were moved by the dream of a far more perfect society than anything that they achieved. Would they have worked with the necessary energy to create the limited reforms if they had not been filled with the illusions? Are illusions necessary to social progress? Niebuhr thinks not. In fact, they are a major cause for the perversion of reform. By self-righteously claiming too much, the reformer fails to guard against the latent evils within his system.

For Niebuhr the answer to the dilemma lies in taking seriously, but not literally, the apocalyptic teaching of the Bible. The apocalyptic teaching of the end of the world and the Second Coming of Christ has been perverted by those who continually forecast the imminent end of the world. But the depth of meaning in them must be kept. The Christian hope for history looks beyond history. God's resources for fulfilling his will are not limited by this world or this life. It is a grave mistake, however, to make Christianity simply an otherworldly religion. Apocalypse teaches that history is fulfilled, not denied. Hence the course of man's history, his victories over evil, have an ultimate importance in the final fulfillment beyond history.

The Christian can work for reform and progress without being filled with illusions. Because he does not expect the Kingdom of God, or the perfect social order, upon this earth, he is not led into the despair into which the secular reformer often falls when the full difficulties of the task come to view. On the other hand, believing that anything which he can do will have significance in the ultimate fulfillment of history, the Christian is driven to action and does what he can even if there is no apparent hope of success.

Niebuhr is often looked upon as a prophet of gloom. It is true that against the background of American optimism he often has spoken sobering words that sounded pessimistic by contrast. But Niebuhr might well reply, as Dean Inge said in answer to those who had called him the "Gloomy Dean," "Things have turned out a lot worse than I prophesied." Niebuhr saw early in his career that both excessive optimism and despair are enemies of the Gospel and he has tried to steer a realistic course between them. In a recent article he has pointed out that the prophets of doom have been proved wrong so far. They had forecast that if we followed certain policies there would be atomic war. But we followed the policies and war did not come. This illustrates for Niebuhr the fact that society is not run by iron laws of necessity. There is a freedom of choice involved, and we can never be certain about what is going to happen in history because man may use his freedom to do what was not foreseen. In this freedom lies the antidote both to despair and to excessive optimism. Because man has a certain freedom, although not absolute freedom, he may ruin a good society. Consequently, we cannot reasonably hope for an enduring

Utopia. On the other hand, man can also use his freedom to improve any situation in which he finds himself. That is why we should never sit quietly in the midst of an evil situation; it can always be improved.

Because of his interpretation of the relationship between Christianity and social life, Niebuhr finds that the Christian may be called to several types of vocation. We need some Christian perfectionists who, like the pacifist, will refuse to compromise with the world and will live by absolute standards. Niebuhr feels that such a person is always partly deluded, for he is not as free from sin as he thinks. He depends upon the evils of society in a host of subtle ways. For example, he cannot buy food without paying taxes which support the war effort or other evil that he opposes. Despite this, the perfectionist forces other Christians to remember the full implications of Jesus' teaching and to realize that they are compromising with evil. He ought to move them to a sense of repentance.

Another Christian may be called to be a prophet who will hold the absolute demands of Christ before society and who will condemn the compromises that society must make. His function is to awaken the conscience of men and to force them to see that they are stained with a guilt that is not unlike that which they condemn in their enemies. Niebuhr has often assumed this role himself.

But a Christian may also be called to become a compromising statesman. He may hold high office in the land or he may be a private in the army. But wherever he is he knows that the perfect life is not a possibility for him. He knows that if he does not compromise and work for the lesser evil, a worse evil will triumph. He does not like the compromise; he constantly seeks the forgiveness of God for it; but he also feels that it is his duty to God to stand where he is and do the best that can be done in a complex situation. The majority of Christians will always be here. But despite the compromise, there is a world of difference between the Christian who accepts the compromise with sorrow and repentance and the man who compromises by accepting the evil as his good. The Christian will ever be alert to find some way to ameliorate the evil that he must do, while the other man will not even be conscious that he is involved in evil.

We might illustrate this difference by pointing with Niebuhr to Lincoln. Lincoln accepted the Civil War as a tragic necessity, the lesser of the two evils from which he had to choose. But because he knew that it was an evil, Lincoln had his heart open to forgive and to rehabilitate at the first opportunity. Over against Lincoln were those who fought what they considered was a righteous crusade and who had no idea that they were compromising. Their hearts were filled with a vindictive desire for vengeance. The difference in attitude made a world of difference for future history.

Niebuhr has, more than any other, raised America above the impasse of the fundamentalist-modernist controversy by daring to see values and errors on both sides. If Americans and Europeans are able to converse with each other in the ecumenical movement, it is partly because Niebuhr has been a mediator between them. There is no doubt that the future of American theology will be decisively changed because of him whether it follows his thinking or not. Before theology can take a line different from Niebuhr, it must come to terms with him. Hardly a book on theology appears today which does not take Niebuhr into serious consideration, even if it comes ultimately to an anti-Niebuhrian point of view. We can prophesy with assurance that he will have a strong following for many years to come.

CHAPTER 8

The Boundary Between Liberalism and Neo-Orthodoxy: Paul Tillich

Paul Tillich holds a place of increasing importance in American theological thought. With the help of Reinhold Niebuhr he fled the tyranny of Hitler in 1933 to become a professor at Union Theological Seminary, New York. Although he is essentially a thinker and scholar, he has led an active life. Four years as a chaplain in World War I impressed him with the depth of social problems. He returned from the war to work with the Religious Socialist movement in Germany, an activity which made existence under Hitler impossible.

Since coming to America, Tillich has spent considerable time working with refugees from Europe. He has been active in the Council for a Democratic Germany. This work has kept him in intimate touch with European developments. Tillich, who likes to stand on the boundary between various points of view, thus stands on the boundary between Europe and America.

Tillich has been called, with good reason, the "theologian's theologian." His writings are never easy reading, although they are singularly rewarding to the reader who perseveres. He brings to his thinking an amazing scholarship. He is completely at home in several fields of thought, including history, philosophy, psychology, art, and political analysis, in addition to his theological specialty.

Tillich is typical of German scholarship at its best. No American theologian has such wealth of historical research behind his thought. He recalls without effort the essence of the thought of even the most obscure thinker of the past. But, also typical of the scholar, he cannot, without the aid of his assistant, recall where he left his lecture notes.

Tillich occupies a strange position in theology. In Europe he is often looked upon as a liberal theologian and an active opponent of Barth and Brunner. He has referred humorously to himself as "the last liberal." But in America he is widely considered as one of the neo-orthodox school, and in some quarters he is even grouped with Barth and Brunner. The best description of him is that he stands upon the boundary between liberalism and neo-orthodoxy, taking the best from both but refusing to be identified with either.

Tillich joins the liberals in their insistence that religion must be subjected to the scrutiny of reason. He accepts wholeheartedly the higher criticism of the Bible and denies the demand of Barth that Christianity be understood apart from secular knowledge. Unlike Barth, also, Tillich believes that God's creative work may still be discerned within nature. On the other hand, Tillich stands with orthodoxy and neo-orthodoxy in his insistence that the final criterion of all revelation is the picture of "Jesus as the Christ" which we find in the Bible. He proclaims the distance between God and man and the danger of idolatry in any thought or action that claims too simply to have found God. He also agrees with orthodox and neo-orthodox concepts of sin.

Tillich's relation to other forms of thought becomes more clear when we examine the "principle of correlation" which he has made central to his theological method. Whereas Barth believes that it is impossible and unfitting to relate the Christian Gospel to the cultural situation and thought of the present, Tillich believes that it is the unavoidable duty of every theologian to relate the biblical message to his contemporary situation. He insists that man cannot receive answers to questions that he has not even asked. Therefore, if man is to understand the revelation of Christ, there must be a preparation which enables him to comprehend revelation. That is, there must be a correlation between the thought and problems of every age and the answers given by religious faith. It is the task of the theologian to demonstrate this correlation. In other words, Christian theology must learn to speak the language of the culture in which it finds itself.

When we turn to Tillich's *Systematic Theology* we find, therefore, first an analysis of a particular problem in terms of modern philosophy. When the problem has been pushed to its final depth and its relation to man's very existence and being becomes clear, Tillich shows how the Christian revelation gives an answer to the problem. The answer is always symbolic and even paradoxical, but it is ultimately more satisfying than any alternative. By thus correlating question and answer, modern thought and biblical revelation, Tillich gives to his thought a far more systematic form than is found in Barth.

Tillich does not imply by his method of correlation that the answers to the problems of life can be deduced from the philosophical analysis of them. The answers are supplied "from beyond." Tillich tries to stand between what he considers to be two false methods. On the one hand, naturalistic philosophy tries to answer questions from the analysis of man's natural existence. This method fails to see that it is man's existence itself which is the question. Liberal theology often makes the error of explaining Christianity as a system developed by man's natural religious tendencies. Christianity thus becomes something that is said by man, not something said to man. On the other hand, Tillich repudiates what he calls the supernaturalistic fallacy which sees the Christian message as a set of sacred truths that "have fallen into the human situation like strange bodies from a strange world."

The method of correlation becomes more clear when we understand three terms that Tillich uses continually: theonomy, heteronomy, and autonomy. All thinking, believes Tillich, is an expression of one or more of these.

Heteronomy is the imposition of a law upon man from outside himself. Heteronomy may appear in religious or secular forms. When a religion sets itself up to dictate belief and action, it is heteronomous. It ignores and destroys all creativity within man; it stifles the expression of man's reason. Heteronomy usually justifies itself by claiming to speak for God. In heteronomy God is pictured as the supreme lawgiver who must be obeyed simply because he demands. Why should we obey such a God? Only, it would seem, says Tillich, because he is more powerful than we. But this is a poor reason, for we destroy ourselves in submitting to such a strange and alien power.

When men have been subjected to a heteronomy, sooner or later they rebel, and usually they rebel in the name of autonomy, the rule of the self by the self. In autonomy one lives by the rational structure of his own mind, making his own laws. The autonomous man is one who refuses to bow before anything outside himself, and who sets out to be the captain of his fate and the master of his soul.

Theonomy repudiates both heteronomy and autonomy. It asserts that the superior law, rooted in God, is at the same time the innermost law of man himself. One does not receive this law from external agencies but finds it within his own heart. The law given by God is thus in harmony with man's own essential nature. It calls man to be what he was meant to be. In obeying the law of God theonomously, one does not destroy himself as when he obeys a heteronomous law; rather he fulfills himself. He finds what he truly is. The commands of God are to be fulfilled, then, not because God has more power than we but because they are the expression of man's essential relation to himself, to others, and to the universe.

As Tillich looks back over history he finds that different historical periods have been characterized by one or the other of these forms. The early Middle Ages and the early Reformation were periods of theonomy when the ultimate depth of life, God, shone through everything. Religion is a natural expression of life in the theonomous period. There is no division of life into sacred and secular, for all life is seen in its relation to the divine. In such a society religion does not stand over man giving him orders; rather it is the lifeblood of one's existence, the presupposition of all thought. Men are not even consciously religious. In theonomous periods men do not feel split; instead they feel whole, centered, and at home in the universe.

When a theonomous period loses its power, it normally sinks into heteronomy. When the religious life is no longer that which comes naturally, the religious authorities try to force men to be religious. Thought must be censored, misdeeds punished, and the law of God enforced by the proper authorities. Thus the late Middle Ages and the later period of the Reformation both developed heteronomies. Orthodoxy became a strict rule to be enforced; religious persecution became common.

The reaction to a heteronomous period is often a period of autonomy. The Renaissance reacted autonomously to the late Middle Ages, and Rationalism, in the eighteenth century, reacted to the heteronomous orthodoxy of later Protestantism. There is no doubt that Tillich welcomes the autonomous revolt; it is perfectly proper against the demands of heteronomy. Autonomy fights heteronomy for the freedom and dignity of the individual. The autonomous period throws aside all external rule. It sets up principles such as "Art for art's sake," "Business is business," and "One man's religion is as good as another's."

Although Tillich applauds the reassertion of autonomy against heteronomy, he finds that the autonomous period cannot satisfy the deeper needs of man. It leaves him without any depth or cohesion in life. We stand today in the midst of a disintegrating autonomous order. An autonomous age loses both its view of the world as a whole and a center to life. Life is split into a series of unrelated activities with no depth or meaning. The autonomous man becomes bewildered, with no direction to life. He is no longer self-assured and creative, but disturbed, frustrated, and often in despair. In short, autonomy gives man no certainty, no security, and no foundation for life.

When an autonomous period breaks down, as it is doing today, it may go in one of two directions. The lure of heteronomy is strong at such a time. Religions of authoritarianism offer man a sense of security and strength if he will give up his autonomous freedom. On the other hand, secular heteronomies arise in the form of totalitarian states, whether Nazi or Communist, offering men the sense of a unified life, a meaningful goal for the future, and above all security. We live in an age that leads many to "escape from freedom." The other alternative is that a new theonomy may arise. Men on the borderline of despair may, instead of abandoning their freedom, find the wholeness, meaning, and depth of life in God. God in such theonomy is not an outside force or power that comes in to rescue man; God is the depth and foundation behind those aspects of truth and goodness which autonomy has already found.

Theonomy is expressed for Tillich in the essential principle of Protestantism. His understanding of Protestantism begins with an analysis of man. Man finds himself faced with a "boundary situation" which arises at the point where everything that makes life meaningful is threatened. It is encountered whenever all human possibility reaches its limit or boundary. At this point existence itself is threatened. This is not to be confused with death, although death may point to man's boundary situation.

The boundary situation is a threat to man because of his freedom. Man does not grow, as does a flower, into his natural form; he has freedom to decide for or against it. He is haunted with the demand to fulfill the good and the true. If this demand is not fulfilled, and it never is, then life is driven into discord, guilt, and ultimately to anxiety. Man tries in various ways to escape this anxiety. He leans upon past success in finding truth or in achieving goodness. He runs to the arms of a heteronomous religion which promises him security. He may throw himself into restless activity or sink in the delights of the flesh. He may try to find his security in totalitarian political movements. At the end of an autonomous era like ours, man is threshing about looking in all directions for salvation from the threat to the meaning and value of his existence.

The anxiety faced at the boundary is not to be identified with fear. Fear is always directed at a specific danger and may be overcome by courage. But anxiety is the underlying and deeper sense of insecurity that comes from realizing that the whole end and meaning of our existence are threatened. So it is that man finds a sense of relief when, for brief periods, he can lose his anxiety in fear of some specific threat to himself. Then he can muster up his courage and face the threat; but this is always a temporary expedient and, sooner or later, he must again find himself on the boundary. Likewise, this anxiety is not to be confused with neurotic fear and anxiety that can be cured by psychotherapy. This anxiety is the mark of human nature as such.

The Protestant principle is the answer of Christianity, says Tillich, to the boundary situation of life. Protestantism grew out of Luther's rediscovery of the biblical message of justification by faith. This is the paradox that man, the unrighteous, is accepted by God as if he were righteous; man, the unholy, is accepted as if he were holy. Man's anxiety and feeling of guilt are overcome when he accepts the fact that God has accepted him as he is. No longer does he need to pretend that he is more than he is; he can face all of the ambiguity of the boundary situation without rationalizing it away. Man's need to deceive himself is removed. Man's whole life is transformed by the acceptance of God.

The faith by which one receives the forgiving grace of God is not less certain knowledge. Faith means being grasped by the sense of the unconditional which is beyond man. In faith one is lifted out of himself; he is gripped by a power not his own. The saint is not a saint because he is good; he is a saint because he has become transparent for that which is more than himself.

Because of its understanding of grace, Protestantism represents the eternally necessary protest against everything that is set up to take the place of God. To Protestantism only God is holy, and no Church, no doctrine, no saint, no institution, no rite, is holy in itself. Each of these is holy only in so far as it may become a symbol that points beyond itself to the divine holiness. Protestantism revolted from the Roman Catholic Church because the latter claimed that it, as an institution, had the power of dispensing God's grace.

The Protestant principle must likewise protest against even a Protestant Church or creed when it claims to speak absolutely for God. Protestantism is in unqualified opposition to all heteronomy. Wherever heteronomy arises in Protestant garb, it is a perversion of Protestantism. The Protestant is thus led to insist on the priesthood of all believers; that is, the grace of God is not channeled through any particular group of ordained men but is open to all. In any given period the Churches may be so closed to God that he has to work through a purely secular movement. Therefore the duty of Protestantism is not to condemn secularism in unqualified terms; rather it is to stimulate the secularists to look more deeply into their thought and to find its ground and depth, to lead them to the awareness of the theonomous nature of their thought and life.

Tillich feels certain that we are living at the end of an era. The social forces and thought forms that have governed life for the past few centuries are in disintegration. The problem of the Protestant Church is that it is so closely identified with the decaying society that it faces the real possibility of dying with the old order. The Protestant principle may have to express itself elsewhere and in opposition to the official Protestant Churches.

For Tillich religion is not a matter of certain beliefs or practices; it cannot be identified with the traditional religions. A man is religious at the point where he is ultimately concerned, and he is ultimately concerned when he experiences the unconditional. The experience of the unconditional is the experience of that which has absolute authority for one, of that before which he bows in humility and awe. Ethical obligation, the striving for truth, and beauty, all have elements of the unconditional in them. An ultimate concern is one that takes precedence over all of the other concerns of life. The ultimate concern grasps a man and lifts him out of himself. To it he says, "Not my will but thy will be done." He gives himself to it with all of his heart and mind and soul and strength. An ultimate concern is total; there is no part of oneself or of one's world that is excluded from it.

When one understands religion in these terms, it is evident that religion is often found among the so-called "irreligious." The atheist usually has an ultimate concern for truth or for some other reality. In fact, says Tillich, we must realize that the atheist may be saved by faith. His atheism may arise from a commitment to, and ultimate concern with, truth. Loyalty to truth will not allow him to believe in the God pictured by a religion. But his loyalty to truth is itself a relationship to God, although the atheist does not recognize it as such.

This definition of religion makes it clear that our problem is not irreligion but false religion. Idolatry, the giving of one's ultimate concern to that which is neither ultimate nor unconditional, is the source of the world's ills. When men give their ultimate concern to their state, their Church, their political party, or any other preliminary concern, the results are destructive and chaotic.

The object of theology is that, and only that, which concerns us ultimately. The conflict of science and theology has occurred either when the theologians tried to pontificate on matters of preliminary concern or when the scientist tried to dictate about ultimate concern. Theology has nothing to say about questions of science, art, history, and so on. The preliminary concerns come into theological consideration only when they become symbols pointing towards the ultimate concern.

Because of the nature of religion, theology can never be simply and purely objective. There are, Tillich insists, areas where the detached and objective approach is most satisfactory. But to apply this method, so satisfactory in the physical sciences, to all fields of knowledge is to be less than truly objective. Unconcerned detachment in matters of religion implies an a priori rejection of the religious demand to be ultimately concerned. Hence it denies the God whom it claims to be approaching objectively.

But, we may ask, what ought to concern us ultimately? Tillich replies, "Our ultimate concern is that which determines our being or non-being." We become ultimately concerned with that which we believe to have the power of destroying or saving our very being. Tillich hastens to point out that he does not have in mind our physical being. Many things threaten or save our physical life without concerning us ultimately. He uses the term "being" to refer to the whole of human reality, the structure, the meaning, and the aim of existence. "To be or not to be" in this sense is a matter of ultimate concern. It penetrates to the very depth of the meaning of life, why we live and for what we live.

In view of the nature of the ultimate concern, Tillich finds that the popular idea of God is not worthy of ultimate concern. This god is but an idol. So Tillich startles his hearers by telling them that he does not believe that God exists. He repudiates the "so-called proofs" for the "so-called existence" of God. This strategy is partly intended to shock his listeners into attention, and it is partly for the sake of more precise terminology.

For Tillich, God does not exist because existence is a category of dependence. A god who exists is simply another being, and even if we call him the supreme being he is still on the same level with ourselves. Superlatives become diminutives when applied to God because they compare God to other beings. This pulls God down to our level even while ostensibly trying to raise him up. Such a god is not worthy of our ultimate concern; he may be more powerful than we, he may be able to blot out our physical existence, but he cannot concern our true existence, the meaning, purpose, and goal of our life. Instead of looking outside nature for a supernatural being called God, Tillich looks through nature to the transcendent depth and ground of nature. God, says Tillich, is not a being, he is Being itself, the power of being which enables all things that are to be.

The history of religion is full of gods. Gods, says Tillich, are beings of superhuman powers. Though they are greater than men, they are images of human nature raised to a superhuman realm. This causes certain skeptics to charge that the gods are only projections of human nature. That is true, says Tillich, but the skeptic forgets that something projected must be projected onto something, a screen. In this case the screen is the experience of a realm that is of ultimate concern.

The sphere of the gods is the sphere of the holy. Holiness is an experienced phenomena. The holy is the quality of that which concerns man ultimately, and only that which is holy can give one ultimate concern. The experience of holiness is normally evoked by some object, and the peril of religion is that the object, which is the occasion of the experience, is taken to be holy itself. Thus arise idolatries in which the objects of religion are considered divine and holy in themselves.

The various attempts to prove the existence of God are perverse, believes Tillich, for they deny God in the very attempt to prove him. Every argument for the existence of God uses God as a missing link to explain the world as we know it. But to call this missing link God is the worst form of atheism. The arguments for the existence of God are not arguments nor are they proofs of God's existence. They are valid only as an analysis of man's situation. Man asks the question about God because he is already aware of God. This awareness is not the result of the argument; it is the presupposition with which it begins. All of the arguments point to the presence of something unconditional within the self and the world. Without this the question would not be asked.

Man faces this unconditional element in the sense of truth. Even the skeptic who says there is no truth has expressed his faith in truth—the truth of his statement that there is no truth. The demand of truth presents itself as unconditional. Man cannot be satisfied with less. Similarly, the sense of ought, the demand to be good, is an unconditional demand. A man may or may not do the good, but he cannot escape the fact that it lays its claims upon him and challenges him.

When we speak of God we must speak, says Tillich, in symbolic terms. The only nonsymbolic statement we can make about God is that he is Being itself. He is not a being but he is that power of being which is within every being enabling it to exist and without which it would cease to exist. Everything else we can say about God is symbolic. For example, we must speak of God as personal, for man cannot be ultimately concerned with anything less than personal. But such a statement is symbolic, for personality implies limitation. It is none the less a fitting symbol, for God is the power of being that underlies all personality and makes it what it is. Similarly, we speak of God causing certain things, but this too is symbolic. God is the basis upon which causality rests, without which there would be neither cause nor effect. But the ground of causation cannot properly be called a cause, not even a First Cause. The world is not something apart from God; it is the medium of his continuing activity.

Faith in God is the answer to the search for a courage that is able to overcome the anxiety that arises from man's boundary situation that we examined earlier. Ordinary courage may overcome the specific threats, but a deeper courage is necessary to overcome the anxiety that arises from the finite nature of life itself. This deeper or ultimate courage is based upon participation in the ultimate power of being. The finitude and the anxiety do not disappear, but the power to live with them is found.

Throughout this discussion of Tillich's view of God, it is evident that Tillich depends upon a deep sense of mysticism. God is experienced as the unconditioned within life. Nature is not simply many objects outside oneself; it is a transparent window through which one can see the reality of God. God is experienced as the sustainer of nature and of oneself —the power from which one draws ultimate courage and a transformation of life. God can never be, therefore, an object beside other objects; he is the depth of reality from which all objects draw their reality.

Tillich combines faith in the finality of revelation in Christ with a sympathetic appreciation of revelation in other religions. The Christian faith that Christ reveals the truth includes the claim that wherever truth appears it is in harmony with Christ. The message of Christ would not have been understood if there had not been a preparation for it. It would have fallen as a strange and meaningless phenomena in a world that had no prior revelation. The religions of man, including the Christian religion, are the preparations enabling man to comprehend the "New Being" that comes in Christ.

Jesus as the Christ was a "New Being" in the sense that he portrayed completely what God meant man to be. Man, as he exists in this world, is not man as God created him to be. This is the meaning of the fall for Tillich; there is a split between the essence of man, what God intended him to be, and what man is existentially (that is, is in reality). In Jesus we find man in complete unity with God, meeting the vicissitudes and temptations of human life but overcoming them with the grace of God. Jesus is not the Christ because of his own power or goodness but because God was present in him. As such the Christian claims that Christ is the final revelation. This does not mean that revelation ceased in the year 33, but it does mean that all revelations are to be tested and weighed by the revelation that comes through Christ.

This claim to finality is justified by Tillich because in Jesus we find a revelation with the power to negate itself without losing itself. Every revelation from the infinite God must come through some medium, but this means that the medium blurs the revelation or in many cases takes the place of the revelation. It is the wonder of Jesus that he gave up all claims for himself; he surrendered everything that was Jesus in him to that which was Christ. That is, Jesus made no personal demands or claims; he pointed continually to God, who worked in and through him. Because Jesus surrendered himself so completely, he became transparent to the mystery that he revealed. Jesus' temptations were the temptations to claim ultimacy for his own finite nature. Jesus steadfastly resisted all temptations to use his union with God for his own advantage.

For Tillich this makes a "Jesus-centered" religion idolatrous. He believes that liberal theology often fell into this error. It is not Jesus the man whom we worship, but the mystery of God that shines through him. Christians do not set up Jesus as a heteronomous authority who demands obedience. Rather in Jesus as the Christ we find the answer to the questions asked in all of men's religions about the relation of man to the ultimate and to his fellow men. In Christ we find not a new law but the true nature of man.

Christianity has no superiority over other religions as a religion. Its people are no more righteous than those of other faiths. But that to which Christianity witnesses, the picture of the Christ, is final.

The revelation of Christ emphasizes love as the law of life. Love in the Christian sense is a power rather than an emotion—the power that reunites that which has been separated. Love combines the sense of an absolute ought with the relativity necessary for particular situations. In every situation in which another person is involved, we ought to treat him with love. But how love will act in any particular situation will depend upon the individual needs of the persons involved. Love is not a heteronomous law; it expresses itself in terms of individual needs.

Tillich notes that whereas a few years ago the dominant problem was the control of nature, today it is the problem of history. Much of his work has been in this field. He finds that though men have freedom in historical situations, there is also a power of destiny that limits the possibilities in any given period. History is going someplace; it has an end and is not a meaningless repetition of events. Within history there is the continual struggle between the forces of good and evil, a struggle that divides both the individual and society. The meaning of history is found in the revelation of Christ.

Tillich has coined a term, *kairos*, to describe the opportunities of history. This is a Greek word used by Paul with regard to Christ and is translated "in the fullness of time." Tillich finds here the concept that the time was ready or prepared for the invasion of history by God through Christ. It was the one unique moment when the revelation was possible. Sooner or later would not have been adequate. As there was the one great *kairos* when Christ came, there are, believes Tillich, smaller *kairoi* throughout history when the time is ripe for particular achievements. The hour of destiny strikes for some new social creation.

The concept of *kairos* enables Tillich to stand between two extremes. On the one hand, he repudiates the pessimist who sees no hope for the future history of man or who believes that no progress is possible. On the other hand, he rejects any form of utopianism which would claim to have built or to be able to build a perfect earthly society. Tillich believes that in the *kairos* a particular gain may be made, a battle with evil won, but that the victory will not be an absolute one over all evils.

It is Tillich's belief that we stand today in a *kairos*. With an era decaying around us, we have an opportunity to build a new theonomous period. In the light of this we can understand his concept of religious socialism. He finds that socialism is acutely aware that we stand in a *kairos* period, that an old age is dying, and that a new one is waiting to be born. Religious socialism is not a political movement; it is an attempt to understand socialism under the light of theonomy. It is as critical of socialism as it is of capitalism. It is not sympathetic either to Marxism or to Communism.

Socialism, says Tillich, sees clearly and rightly the evils of capitalism, the injustices, unemployment, and mechanization of the worker. But socialism fails to go deeply enough in its criticism. Like the capitalists, socialists hope to change society simply by changing techniques and strategy. Like capitalism, socialism tends to make the highest possible increase in economic welfare into its all-determining goal. In this way socialism becomes but the other side of the coin of capitalism, the competitor of capitalism, but not its true alternative.

Tillich's religious socialism tried to understand the divine ground of the social and economic situation. On the other hand, it realized, as much orthodox Christianity did not, that the social conditions of an era can be a real hindrance to the spiritual welfare of man. It also recognized that, to an alarming extent, Protestantism had become the religious aspect of capitalism. The proletariat were estranged from the Protestant Church. Religious socialism set itself the task of winning the proletariat by accepting all that was just and true in the socialist philosophy and pointing to the deeper truths missed by secular socialism. On the other hand, it criticized the utopianism that was evident in socialism. For the religious socialist the *kairos* of socialism has come, but socialism is not and could not be the Kingdom of God or the perfect and final social order. The failure of Marxian Communism to understand this is in large part responsible for its falling into a new and demonic form of heteronomy.

Tillich is a deep and complex thinker. He can no more be summarized in one chapter such as this than can an encyclopedia. It can only be hoped that we have pointed to something of the uniqueness, breadth, and depth of his thought. For several years Tillich made little impression on American theology. This was no doubt due to the fact that he published little and found the language barrier formidable. But in recent years several of Tillich's works have been published and he has been winning a considerable following, particularly among the younger theologians. For at least one thing America can be thankful to Hitler: he was responsible for Paul Tillich's coming to this country.

CHAPTER 9

Orthodoxy As a Growing Tradition

There is a tendency in this country to believe that, theologically speaking, a man has to be fundamentalist, liberal, or neo-orthodox. And neo-orthodox usually means Barthian. But there is a growing number of theologians who are seeking a way between the extremes.

It is not easy to find a suitable name for this mediating school, and there is no name associated with the movement as liberalism or neo-orthodoxy are associated with their movements. Many of its representatives are inclined simply to say that they represent orthodox Christianity. Perhaps the best description would be to say that they accept orthodoxy as a growing tradition. For convenience I will refer to this movement as "modern orthodoxy."

When W. M. Horton was at the beginning of his revolt against the old liberalism, he wrote a book, *Contemporary English Theology*. In it, he pointed out that England had seen the crisis of liberalism in 1907, some twenty-five years before the crisis came in America. The movement "beyond modernism" was well under way in England before the First World War. Horton speculated that England was a forecast of the way in which American theology would go. Today one finds that there is a real movement toward modern orthodoxy in America, but the main interpreters of this school are perhaps still English.

Although we speak of modern orthodoxy as a mediation between extremes, it must not be thought that the position is arrived at by first weighing the modern movements in theology and then taking the best out of each. The heart of this movement lies in loyalty to the faith of historic orthodoxy, not because it is ancient or orthodox but because it is believed to be true. Modern orthodoxy believes that in the orthodox tradition we have a precious heritage of truth which must not be thrown overboard just because someone has split the atom and someone else has looked farther through a telescope. Nevertheless, it is willing to understand the old truth more fully in so far as modern thought makes that possible.

From the point of view of modern orthodoxy, the other groups we have studied represent deviations to the right or left of orthodoxy. It recognizes that each deviation has expressed some truth of orthodoxy but feels that it has done so at the expense of other truths. It recognizes in fundamentalism a concern to protect orthodoxy, but it does not believe that this can be accomplished by freezing it into the thought forms of the past. The doctrine of the verbal inspiration of the Bible is viewed by modern orthodoxy as a deviation from the traditional position of orthodoxy. Though modern orthodoxy welcomes the liberal concern to re-express the ancient truths in terms that the modern world can comprehend, it feels that liberals often lost the truth along with the ancient forms of expression.

Modern orthodoxy agrees with liberalism that reason

must be used in religious thinking. It considers that Barth's denial of natural theology is another deviation from the orthodox tradition. It accepts the critical study of the Bible and has provided some of our best biblical scholars. But it takes more seriously than liberalism the orthodox belief that there is a special revelation through the Bible, that Jesus is the unique incarnation of God, and that man is inherently sinful. It feels that liberalism overemphasizes God's immanence and that Barth overemphasizes God's transcendence. It welcomes liberalism's emphasis upon following the ethical teachings of Jesus but feels that liberals did not weigh realistically the problems that arise when man tries to do this and that consequently they did not see the full need for God's grace in living the ethical life.

Of the groups discussed so far, modern orthodoxy is closest to Niebuhr and neo-liberalism. When George Hammar, the Swedish theologian, made a study of American theology, he did not present his own position, but we catch some glimpse of it in his critique of other positions. He is not Barthian, although he has sympathy with some of Barth's points. He has an almost equal distaste for liberalism and fundamentalism. He finds himself closest to Niebuhr, and finds that neo-liberalism is moving in the "right" direction although its promise is as yet unfulfilled. This attitude is typical of modern orthodoxy.

Modern orthodoxy is, like liberalism, a wide field, and differences of emphasis are to be found within it. What we have to say about it will not necessarily describe any of its members adequately. It is interesting to notice that within this group we can detect both a Protestant and an Anglo-

Catholic approach. These two would agree in their views of Christ, the place of reason, and the essential truth of the early creeds of the Church; but they break company over the doctrines of the Church, the sacraments, and the ordination of the clergy.

One of the contributions of modern orthodoxy is to the doctrine of revelation. From Barth it learned that the liberals and fundamentalists had been fighting over the wrong question. They had been concerned with *how* God is revealed in the Bible. But Barth turned attention to the question "*What* is revealed in the Bible?" It is by answering this question that modern orthodoxy comes to a solution that is implicitly present in Augustine and Luther, although now clarified by biblical criticism.

Modern orthodoxy would assert that God does not reveal theories or doctrines. As Hammar says, in the exact sense there is no such thing as revealed theology, for God does not reveal theology. To speak of a revealed theology over against natural theology is simply to mean a theology that begins with revelation as a fact. Bishop Aulen of Sweden says that while Christian faith is conscious of having a true knowledge of God, it does not mean that it has certain ideas or doctrines about a being called God. Modern orthodoxy realizes that revelation is the act of God whereby he reveals his own being and nature to man. To the question "What does God reveal?" modern orthodoxy answers, "God reveals himself."

To illustrate further, let us follow the late Archbishop of Canterbury, William Temple. He begins by pointing out that if God is not in some sense personal, then we can have no revelation at all. But if he is personal, then we must suppose that there will be both a general and a special revelation. A person reveals his inner nature through his habitual acts day by day. But there come particular moments when, because of circumstances, he reveals much more of his true nature. Thus a man, known to his fellow office workers five days a week, will be known in one way. But if one of those workers is with him while a child is drowning, he will see a completely different side of the man's character, heroic or cowardly as the case may be. The response to such an extraordinary situation will often be such that even one who has known him well will say, "I did not know that he had it in him."

Temple feels that God's revelation is like that. There is a general revelation of God in everything that is. Against Barthianism, Temple asserts the general nature of God's revelation, for all creation must bear the marks of its Creator. Unless all existence is a medium of revelation, no particular revelation is possible. "Only if God is revealed in the rising of the sun in the sky, can he be revealed in the rising of a Son of Man from the dead." But over against any liberals who deny special revelation, Temple asserts that this is to deny God's personality. That is, it denies that God is able to accommodate himself to special or unique situations and needs.

Special revelation does not, insists Temple, give us new truths or put into our minds new ideas. He turns again to Luther, who believed that the Word of God is a living utterance of the living God spoken through, rather than contained in, the Bible. Its divine quality is vindicated by the testimony of the Holy Spirit in the heart and conscience of the believer.

When we turn to the Bible, says Temple, we do not find a series of propositions to believe; rather we find the record of a series of events which are interpreted by men who felt illuminated by faith in God. There are thus always two sides to revelation: the objective event and the subjective interpretation of the event. Behind both event and the interpreting mind is the will of God. We may trace the historical development of the event; we may trace the psychology of the interpreting mind; but these do not exhaust the significance of the event. God, who is behind all, is working through both to fulfill his purpose of revealing himself to man.

The supreme revelation is given in the life and person of Jesus. The revelation is not his teaching or his acts but himself. We see through the Gospels how he inspired those who saw and knew him. The episodes told in the Bible represent a small fraction of his total life, but they are revealing events in which the full nature of his personality comes through. This is important. Christianity is not a dedication to a system of rules or of thought, but a dedication to a person. This is unique among the religions of the world. Other religions have failed to grow with the times. Either they have been outgrown or they have kept their cultures stagnant because they offer a fixed way of life. At certain times Christianity has been captured by conservatism, but it has been untrue to its nature when it was. There is no change of circumstances that can make allegiance to the spirit of a person out of date. Allegiance to Jesus means allegiance to selfless love, and such a spirit is relevant to all times and places.

In revelation we come to know God himself as a living reality in our lives. The true response to revelation is personal loyalty, the commitment of our lives to the God who reveals himself in and through Jesus. This is the primary aspect of revelation from which come the doctrines by which men try to express it. Temple does not disparage doctrines; they are of great importance. False doctrines make it impossible to know the living God fully; good doctrines can aid in this knowledge. But the doctrines are secondary; the revelation and the power of it over our hearts and lives are primary.

It is obvious that modern orthodoxy has room for a rational defense of Christianity and its revelation. This possibility arises from Temple's argument that there is a revelation of God in all things. It is interesting to compare Temple's Gifford Lectures, *Nature, Man, and God*, with Barth's lectures in the same series, *The Knowledge of God.* Barth begins by pointing to the problem for him raised by the requirements of the series. The series was founded for the purpose of expounding and promoting natural theology, independent of all historical religions, as a strict natural science like chemistry and astronomy. Barth finds that he does not believe either in the possibility or in the desirability of such natural theology. Inasmuch as the invitation to Barth was reaffirmed in the light of his objection, Barth asks how he can keep the spirit of the stipulation. He decides that natural theology has been influential only when it has had a strong revealed theology against which it could assert itself.

Therefore, concludes Barth, the greatest service he can perform for natural theology is to put forward in uncompromising terms a theology of revelation to form a background against which natural theology can react. On the other hand, Temple enters fully into the spirit of the series and, drawing upon natural science and secular philosophy, lays a rational ground for belief in God. None the less, Temple makes it clear that such a natural theology is only, so to speak, the anteroom for a theology of revelation, but an anteroom that is both important and necessary.

An increasing number of modern orthodox thinkers are reinterpreting the relation of reason and revelation by finding new meaning in Augustine's insights on this subject. Augustine asked what reason is, and found it to be the instrument by which man organizes, interprets, and comes to understand his experience. That is, experience must precede reason. Christian thought is not the process by which we attain Christianity; it is the way in which we understand and express it. Theology is faith seeking to understand itself.

Not only does experience precede reason, but before we can reason about the facts of experience we must have some presupposed framework within which we interpret the facts. A fact is never just a fact; it must always be interpreted before it is meaningful. C. S. Lewis tells us that the only person he knows who has seen a ghost continues to doubt survival after death. Her set of presuppositions forced her to conclude that the "fact" of "seeing" the ghost must have been an illusion.

Science itself must presuppose certain things in order to do its work. Science cannot prove that there is a world exterior to our minds which can be known by our minds; it presupposes it. Similarly, science presupposes the uniformity of nature. The uniformities discovered by science only prove the uniformity of all nature if the scientist can presuppose them to be a reliable sample of nature as a whole. That is, he "proves" the uniformity of nature by assuming nature to be uniform.

Truth itself depends upon certain presuppositions. That man can know the truth and that it is a valuable thing to know are presuppositions. No amount of reason could prove this, for to prove it we must presuppose it. To many people these presuppositions are taken for granted, but in every age there have been skeptics who denied both. In the modern totalitarian countries we find whole societies organized on this skepticism. "Truth" becomes whatever the rulers choose to call true, and it is valuable only in so far as it suits their ends. The early Christian fathers were not obscurantists when they said, "I believe in order that I may know"; they were analyzing the nature of all knowledge. We must have faith in the possibility and value of truth before we can find it.

All of this is true of reason in general but it is particularly true, as Alan Richardson points out, when we deal with the philosophies by which men live. Every philosophical system must employ a value judgment about what is important or what are the decisive facts. Facts do not speak for themselves until they have been weighed and judged within some framework. As one tries to form a philosophy of life, he is bombarded with an almost infinite number of facts, and often they contradict one another. Before one can draw a conclusion from these facts, he must decide which are most significant. This is a value judgment, and it depends not simply upon reason but upon a man's total reaction to life. It cannot be achieved by looking at the facts because it is the principle by which the facts are selected, weighed, and evaluated. It is the presupposition or "faith principle" with which we begin our thinking.

Christian faith is not different from other philosophies by which men live. Each must have its "faith principle" which, no matter how self-evident it may seem to its believers, is not self-evident to others. Christianity is different only in that it honestly admits its faith instead of hiding it. Thus it becomes clear that we must reject the charge that the unbeliever looks at religion coldly and objectively while the believer is prejudiced. As a matter of fact, both look at it with a set of value judgments and presuppositions which are without proof. E. T. Ramsdell points out that for some people nothing is significant unless it is proved by the scientific method. And since such people usually do not believe religion to be so proved, they reject it. But, says Ramsdell, although a man may know what he can scientifically verify, he cannot know that what is scientifically unverifiable is insignificant; he can only believe it. Yet this belief determines his outlook on the world and the categories by which he seeks to understand it. He has, implicitly or explicitly, presupposed that the natural forces of the world form the ultimate category, and he can only "prove" this because his presupposition considers "insignificant" any facts which seem to point elsewhere.

Richardson goes on to emphasize that truth, in the biblical

sense, is not something that we can know as we know about electrons or square root. We know about God only by acting, as we know about love only by loving. Thus, says Richardson, unlike Barth and Brunner, the Bible and classical Christian theologians do not distinguish sharply between Christian and pagan knowledge of God. Anyone, pagan or Christian, who has known God through the doing of his will has known him truly, even if his knowledge may have been incomplete.

This interpretation of reason is offered as a solution to the problem of reason and faith. Liberalism, and Roman Catholic thought, in so far as it follows Aquinas, have tended to believe that we can start with reason. By reason we can prove certain things. When we have carried reason as far as it can go, we go beyond it in faith. The Catholic, believing that he has an infallible revelation, can be even more certain of that which he knows by faith than of that which he knows by reason. But the liberal, lacking any infallible revelation, must always be less sure of his faith than he is of his reason. For both it is important that reason be able to prove the existence of God so that faith can have a rational basis. One of the problems of this approach is that equally rational men come to opposite conclusions upon the ultimate questions. For example, proofs of God have divided the great philosophers about equally into those who accept and those who reject the arguments. Reason would seem to have given us something less than certainty.

An alternative view is to start with faith which is its own proof, and anything in reason which contradicts it must be wrong. For Kierkegaard and Barth faith is in a realm hermetically sealed so that no facts could dislodge it. The danger of this approach is that it easily becomes dogmatic and flies in the face of facts or reason.

The Augustinian approach tries to solve this dilemma. It recognizes that we start with a faith, a basic set of presuppositions and evaluations. Without such presuppositions reason is impossible. Such a beginning does not, however, lead to dogmatism, for all facts are to be examined. Reason is to be employed as thoroughly as the Thomist or liberal applies it. But it is recognized that reason, particularly when dealing with the basic and ultimate issues of life, and not with electrons or square roots, will reach the true conclusions only if it starts with the true set of presuppositions and value judgments. This explains why the most competent philosophers have always been sharply divided into mutually exclusive schools of thought without being able to refute each other. Each group can usually iron out the inconsistencies in its system, but it cannot persuade the philosopher who begins with a different framework of presuppositions and value judgments. This explains the failure of philosophers to agree upon the certainty of the proofs of God. We must conclude that God and other tenets of religion cannot be "proved" by reason unless reason is first illuminated by truth. Even in reasoning we are saved by faith.

From this viewpoint we come to see that Christianity does not supply a complete metaphysics or world view. It does give us a new perspective, a new set of values through which we see the facts in a truer light. As A. N. Whitehead says, the dogmas of religion are the attempts to formulate truths disclosed by the religious experience of man just as the dogmas of physical science are the attempt to formulate the truths discovered by the sense perceptions of man. In neither case do the dogmas produce the experience.

At first sight this may seem to lead to a deplorable relativism. If our philosophy of life depends upon starting with a set of presuppositions, how can we ever find truth? Must we not admit that one set of presuppositions is as good as another? By what process do we prefer the Christian "faith principle" to that of Marx or Hitler? Richardson answers this by pointing out that we ought to accept that presupposition or point of view from which we can see most clearly, coherently, and rationally all of the facts of life without having to explain any of them away. At this point he believes that the Christian point of view proves its superiority.

Personally, it seems to me that this approach will remove many of the objections to theology which one finds in laymen and, for that matter, in the clergy itself. To both groups it often seems that theology is an ivory-tower pursuit, in which a group of intellectuals sit apart from life and become involved in disputes over highly technical points of abstract reasoning. But with this Augustinian interpretation it is clearly recognized that the living of Christianity is primary. Before thought there comes the experience of being a Christian. Theology is not a pursuit divorced from the practical demands of life; it is the result of thinking through the problems that arise as we live. Theology is neither the attempt to demonstrate with abstract logic the existence of God, as if we were certain of our logic but uncertain of God, nor is it an attempt to use God as a theory to explain certain problems about the universe. Theology becomes thinking about life and its problems in light of the fact that one is a Christian. It is the attempt to demonstrate the clarity, coherence, and meaning that one finds in life when he begins with the Christian point of view.

This approach is true both to history and to psychology. The first Christians were not argued into Christianity by abstract logical deductions. They found that in their relation to Jesus they had their eyes opened. That is, from their life with him they came to a new set of basic presuppositions and value judgments. This is still true of the man who becomes a Christian today.

One of the concerns of modern orthodoxy has been to reestablish Christology, that is, the doctrine about Christ. D. M. Baillie, in his book *God Was in Christ*, gives what is probably a typical defense of this attitude. He first emphasizes that since the gains of liberalism we can no longer deny that Jesus was truly a man. He notes further that for many persons this "Jesus of history" is enough. For many the beauty of character, the moral power, the sublimity of teaching that are found in Jesus are enough to lay the foundation for a religion. To them it adds nothing but mystification to bring in doctrines about Jesus' divinity. In man's age-old search for the divine, Jesus is the great pioneer and explorer. Is it not enough to honor him as such and is it not better to follow him than to pay him theological compliments by calling him divine? This attitude, notes Baillie, does not have much following among theologians today, but it is popular amongst some of the finest and most sincere laymen.

Baillie answers the objector to Christology by asking first a question. "What do we mean by 'God' if we say that Jesus is the great discoverer of God?" It is imperative to see that

Christology is not an attempt to penetrate into the psychological workings of Jesus' mind; it is basically a question about the nature of God, not about the nature of Jesus. If Jesus discovered God, what kind of God did he discover? Baillie asks, Did Jesus discover a God who would wait to be discovered? And to this he answers, "No."

Baillie justifies this by pointing out that the Jewish scholar C. Montefiore has demonstrated that, when compared with Judaism, there is only one teaching that we find in Jesus but do not find in any Jewish teaching before his time. That is the teaching that God is like a shepherd who goes out to seek the lost sheep. Jews always believed that God was a God of love and forgiveness and that, if the sinner repented, God would freely forgive him. But Jesus taught that God would not wait for the sinner to repent; he would go out and seek the sinner to call him back.

Now we must ask, says Baillie, What was God doing while men were seeking for him? If he merely sat in heaven, waiting to be found, he is not the kind of God that Jesus said he was. If Jesus is only the man who discovered more about God than any other, he failed miserably. At the one point where Jesus was most original in teaching about God, he proves to be wrong. God was not seeking the lost, as Jesus taught; he was waiting to be discovered. In short, says Baillie, if we do not have a doctrine about Jesus, we cannot accept Jesus' doctrine about God.

Baillie calls it illusory to suppose that it is simple to believe in the God and Father of Jesus but that it is difficult to believe in the divinity of Jesus. It is illusory because, if we have no concrete example of God seeking man, how can we believe that he is, as Jesus says, a seeking God? Belief in the divinity of Jesus is the sole way in which the Christian belief in God can be made credible. We do not say simply that God is like Christ, although that is partly true; rather we say that God was *in* Christ. Christ is the activity of God, God at work in the world seeking to save that which is lost. Thus the question "Who is Jesus?" is another way of asking, What is the true nature of God? In the New Testament, Baillie notes, the writers do not speak so much of the love of Christ as they speak of the love of God which is found at work in Christ.

In this light we can understand the Trinitarian and Christological controversies in the early Church. They were not haggling over some vague metaphysical concept. They were earnestly asking whether God's desire to seek and to save man was a part of his nature. When the Arians made Jesus less than God, although more than man, they were, in effect, denying that God's desire to save man was a part of his essential nature. Salvation was the work of a lesser, though divine, being. Orthodox Christians denied this because it implied that God was not sufficiently interested in man's salvation to work for it himself; he left the task to a subordinate.

The doctrine of the Incarnation is that which expresses the Christian faith that God dwelt in Jesus in a unique manner. When Baillie turns to describe the nature of the Incarnation, he may not take the whole modern orthodox school with him, but he is typical in the way in which he tackles the problem.

The central paradox of the Christian faith, says Baillie, is the experience of every believer that he acts freely and yet knows that the good which he does is in reality the work of God's grace. This amazing fact is demonstrated by the witness of Christian life through the ages and is recognized by every Christian. God puts demands upon us that only God, working through us, can perform. We are indeed most free precisely in the moment when God is most in control of our lives. This paradox, never understood by the moralist, is the very heart of the Christian faith. It is, of course, this aspect of Christian life which Augustine and Calvin tried to express in terms of predestination. But predestination is too rational a system to express it; it does not do justice to the freedom and responsibility that are involved.

To some readers, what Baillie is talking about will be quite clear. None the less, I should like to use an illustration from another field to point to an analogous paradox. A few years ago there was a light-hearted motion picture called *I Married a Witch.* The theme of the film was centered upon a beautiful blond witch who had a magic potion by which she forced a man to fall in love with her. As time passed, she became dissatisfied with this compulsory love and ceased administering the brew in order that the man might come to love her freely. This theme points up the paradox of human love. We cannot be satisfied with a love that is compelled; we desire the other to love us freely. But at the same time love is not a free act. No man, by an act of will, falls in love. In fact, the phrase "fall in love" implies the truth that it is not a simple voluntary act. It is paradoxical. It loses its value if it is forced upon a person, and yet it is not something which the person is free to do or not to do as he pleases. I know of no better analogy for the Christian experience of grace. It would be meaningless if God forced himself upon us with some kind of supernatural power, like a witch's potion. Whenever the doctrine of predestination implies that, it is not true to the facts. But, on the other hand, one falls into grace as much as he falls into love.

In the paradoxical experience of grace, Baillie suggests, we have a key to Christology. It does not explain the Incarnation, but it keeps it from being a mystery that has no relation to our experience. Even as we do good because God is at work within us, so Jesus gave full credit to God for all that was good in him. What other men have known spasmodically and imperfectly, Christ knew completely and perfectly. When we look at the picture of Jesus in the Bible we find that he makes great claims for himself, but even in making them he disclaims that *he* has accomplished great things. It is to God that he gives the glory. The God-man is thus he who claims nothing for himself and all for God.

If someone asks if any man who lived a perfect life could be God incarnate, Baillie answers that this is a Pelagian question. When we really understand the paradox of grace, "I . . . yet not I, but God," we find that such a question is meaningless. Jesus is not the incarnate God because he was so good; he was good because God dwelt in him. Thus we are able to proclaim that Jesus was fully as human as we are and that at the same time God was in him as he was not and is not in any other. In Jesus God was acting to fulfill his desire to reveal himself to man so that he might redeem man. Because the grace of God portrayed itself perfectly in Christ, it can portray itself imperfectly in others.

Whereas fundamentalism makes the Atonement central,

modern orthodoxy tends to make the Incarnation central. Fundamentalism is committed to one view of atonement—the substitutionary death of Christ for the sins of man. Modern orthodoxy is, in line with historic Christianity, hesitant to make any doctrine of atonement final. The result is that the death of Jesus is of central importance for fundamentalism, while modern orthodoxy, like liberalism, looks to the whole life of Jesus. In particular, modern orthodoxy emphasizes that the Resurrection of Jesus cannot be separated from his atoning work.

Gustaf Aulen has suggested a return to the classical doctrine of the Atonement. The reader will recall that this is the doctrine which held sway for the first thousand years of Christianity and which taught that God, through the death of Jesus, defeated Satan and freed man from Satan's clutches. Aulen argues persuasively that this is the doctrine of the New Testament itself. It would be strange indeed if the Bible taught the fundamentalist or Anselmic doctrine and if for the first thousand years of Christianity no one recognized it. Aulen feels that the classical doctrine was discredited because it was presented too mythically. We must find new ways to express it, but the heart of it must be retained. It is a persuasive doctrine to many modern orthodox thinkers because it combines the Incarnation and Atonement.

The essence of this doctrine, says Aulen, lies in emphasizing that the Atonement, the bringing of God and man together, is God's work through and through. The Anselmic views are always in danger of picturing Jesus as doing something to make God willing to forgive. The classical doctrine sees clearly that God not only plans but himself performs the work. Sin had obtained a power and control over man which kept him from God. God, incarnate in Christ, met the forces of evil and overcame them, not by sheer power, but by giving himself over into their power, by allowing himself to be crucified. But the forces of evil were unable to hold their initial victory, for Christ arose from the dead. The decisive battle in the war with evil had been fought and won by God. A new relation of God and man was made possible.

The Devil is the mythological means of expressing the belief that God is in final control of the world. The Devil is at once the rebel against God and God's own method of punishing evil. The Devil owes his power and being to God. That is, there is no evil power independent of God; evil is always corrupted goodness. The defeat of the Devil implies the faith that, because of its nature, evil always overreaches and defeats itself.

This doctrine has been expressed vividly in J. S. Stewart's book *A Faith to Proclaim.* The original teaching of Christians was not, Stewart points out, a theory about God but a doctrine of salvation. They proclaimed that God had entered into history and had acted to defeat and overcome the powers of evil. This was the significance of the healing of the sick, the return to sanity of those possessed by demons, and the conversion of sinners. All of these events pointed to the central fact that evil had met its match, a new age had dawned, new hope was available for man. Similarly today, the greatest witness for the Gospel is men and women whose lives have received new power and who are living triumphant over the sins that formerly bound them.

Stewart insists that we have to take seriously the biblical teaching about Satan and the demons, the forces that war against God. Granted that these symbols may have been too mythological, they none the less pointed to something real in life. Men today find themselves gripped by Fate, by a power beyond themselves. Hiroshima and Nagasaki stand as symbols of the lengths to which men and nations of an average decent morality are compelled to go. We find that there is in truth "another law in my members, warring against the law of my mind" (Rom. 7:23).

Jesus came into the world as one who advances into enemy-occupied territory. He allowed himself to be put under the control of the forces of evil knowing that they would overreach and thus defeat themselves. The powers of evil which crucify Christ are made to fulfill the will of God. The complete rule of God over all things is thus manifested.

In this view, the Resurrection is not a mere epilogue to the Gospel. When Christ arose from the dead, it was not simply an announcement that there is a life hereafter. It was the shattering of history by the creative act of God. It begins a new era for the universe, a decisive turning point for the human race. To men held in the grip of fear and futility, to men who see only the blind laws of nature grinding on their way, foredooming man to his fate; to men who see no hope for the future of mankind, the Resurrection proclaims the fact that there is a power at work in the world which is mightier than all the forces that crucified our Lord. The Resurrection is not just a personal survival of the man Jesus, a phenomenon to be studied by the Society for Psychical Research; it is a cosmic victory. Furthermore, it is a victory that can be shared by men. To those enslaved by passion, crushed and disillusioned, the promise comes, "You can share Christ's risen life!" The God who raised Christ from the dead will not find your problem too difficult to handle. It can be overcome by a vital relationship with the living and resurrected Christ. This is the true atonement, the making at one of man and God.

One of the themes of modern theology has been a new concern for the Church. We saw some of the reasons for this when we were treating neo-liberalism. The ecumenical movement, in which Protestant Churches are trying to find a new unity, has forced Protestants to ask seriously the question What is the Church, its purpose, its nature? But the ecumenical movement is itself, in part, the result of the new concern for the Church. This renewed emphasis on the Church is partly due to the secular nature of our age. When so many sections of modern life feel that they can get along quite well without Christianity, it is only natural that Christians should reconsider the center from which Christianity is proclaimed—the Church. Furthermore, the fact that this secularism has arisen in some countries to persecute the Church, as it has not been persecuted for many centuries, has had its effect. The heroism with which the Church met this persecution, and the fact that it was often only the Church that opposed totalitarianism, have led Christians to a new respect for it. In the face of militant secularism, it is clear that no Christian can stand alone. In addition to all of this, biblical criticism has revealed that it was Christ's intention to found a Church, a fellowship of his followers. It can no longer be thought about as an accidental result of Jesus' life and work.

In keeping with this concern of modern theology, modern orthodoxy has insisted upon the unity of the Church. The problem of the ecumenical movement is not to make the Church one; it already is one. The problem is to get the denominations to recognize this unity. Unity lies in the fact that there is one Lord, one head, one faith, one baptism. The division of the Church into denominations may obscure, but it cannot repudiate this fact.

For modern orthodoxy, life in the Church is life in the new age. It is fellowship with Christ and his followers in a living community. There is a truth in the statement that outside the Church there is no salvation. If the Church is thought of as those who serve and follow Christ, then it is evident that one does not come to Christ except through those who are witnessing to him. Further, the motivation to love that is found in Christ moves one to join the community of love, the Church.

This is not to say that modern orthodoxy is uncritical of the Church. It is aware that the Church has borne Christ's name all too often when it failed to express his spirit. Protestant members of the group have called upon the Church to repent; but Anglo-Catholics have objected, saying that the Church, the Body of Christ, cannot repent, although its members need to repent for having failed the Church. Often this conflict seems, however, to be one of terminology rather than of substance. Behind it lies the tendency of Protestants to emphasize the human nature of the Church and of Anglo-Catholics to emphasize its divine nature.

Both Protestant and Catholic representatives of modern orthodoxy would agree that the Church is, in some sense, a divine institution. It is not just a gathering of men who happen to be like-minded. It is not to be explained in sociological terms alone. It is the community which owes its existence to the act of God. It is founded in, and continues to express, the Incarnation. The existence of the Church is the reminder that God has spoken to man and that he continues to speak. The Church stands on the borderline of time and eternity. It has, so to speak, one foot in the world, with all of its problems; but the other foot is planted firmly in eternity and from there it draws the strength to fight its battles in the world.

Modern orthodoxy cannot be said to have any one position upon the relation of Christianity to social and political problems. There is, however, a deep concern with them. William Temple, for example, will long be remembered for his active participation in the political affairs of England, his prophetic leadership of the Church in its pronouncements upon social and political questions, and his radical criticism of the economic and political *status quo*.

Again we find that modern orthodoxy is a mediation between other theologies. It has renounced the optimism of the liberal social gospel. It does not believe that any one social organization can be considered *the* Christian society or solution. It is almost as afraid as is Niebuhr of Utopian schemes. On the other hand, it is more hopeful than Barthianism that real advances can be made in the social life of man. It agrees with Barth that the final hope for man is the hope for the fulfillment of life beyond history. But it denies that this is the only hope; there is a real hope for a better, though not perfect, society upon earth. We might say that where Barth and Niebuhr speak of the "impossible possibility" of the Christian ethic, modern orthodoxy inclines to speak of a "possible impossibility."

One of the most significant things about modern orthodoxy is the appeal that it has for laymen. Our age is witnessing the rebirth of theology written by laymen, men and women whose work and fame lie in other fields. The most prominent of these are C. S. Lewis, Dorothy Sayers, Herbert Butterfield, and Chad Walsh. In each case these lay writers have found their way to a modern orthodox position, repudiating fundamentalism and liberalism as twin perversions of the faith and showing an evidence of bewilderment about neo-orthodoxy. But they have found spiritual enlightenment in a reinterpretation of the orthodox tradition. Natural theology is a vital part of their thought. We recall C. S. Lewis's many proofs of God; but in each case they come to an undiluted theology of revelation through the God-man, Jesus Christ.

This summary of modern orthodoxy reveals its central nature as a mediating movement in theology and its wish to stand in the main tradition of Christian belief and practice. The ecumenical movement has given it considerable power. The ecumenical movement is slowly and painfully working out an ecumenical theology. Its lines are essentially those which we have described as modern orthodoxy. Europe, with its Barthian outlook, and America, with its strong liberal or neo-liberal attitudes, are poles apart. But between them there has grown up a middle way, a theology which finds truth in both sides and which, in some cases, is acceptable both to Barthians and to liberals.

CHAPTER 10

Conclusion

The wide varieties of theological thought which we have surveyed may seem deplorable to the reader. Perhaps he has the feeling of being lost in a maze of conflicting ideas. He may feel as many voters feel on the eve of an election: he has listened to the conflicting parties present their views and now he is completely confused about how to vote. And yet, that is the essence of democracy. If there were only one totalitarian party he would not have to choose. I believe that the same principle holds in theology. The varying viewpoints of theology, although uncomfortable to the man who wants a simple and easy choice, are the very lifeblood of a vital religious life. If there were no such differences we would have totalitarian religion. Protestantism must consider its differences as its glory and not its shame. Of course, where the differences lead to intolerance and slander, we need to repent. But even then we repent, not for our difference in views, but for our failure to love one another in our differences.

There is a further similarity to the political scene. In an election campaign one hears little of the great realm of ideas which two political parties hold in common. The purpose of the campaign is to bring out differences. If the parties were face to face with a totally alien philosophy, such as Communism or Nazism, the great area of agreement would become apparent. The reader must remember that this book is like a political campaign. It has not pictured Christians over against their anti-Christian foes. If it had done that, it would have dwelt on the large areas of agreement. Rather it has pictured Christians thinking out the meaning of Christian faith along with their fellow Christians, and we have tried to bring out their distinctive positions. Furthermore, it must not be supposed that the lines between the schools of thought are always as sharp and clear as I have tended to make them. There is many a Christian who cannot be pushed into any one of the categories that I have found. These divisions simply point to tendencies and trends in modern Christian thought. Neither must the reader conclude that these various schools can never work together, for they do continually in many of our denominations and in the ecumenical movement. As long as they discuss with Christian love, their differing positions will be of help to one another in finding the truth about life in general and Christianity in particular.

Differences of thought must be very perturbing to the man who believes that he has a set of precise doctrines revealed by God. If one believes this then he must believe that all who disagree with him are wrong. The only answer to the man who denies this final truth is to cry "anathema" or "heretic."

But if we take the position that human truth is always finite, we must welcome difference. If we believe that infallibility is never attained in human affairs, we must welcome diversity of thought as a needed corrective of our own limitations.

I do not wish to be misunderstood here. I am not advocating that sloppy idea of tolerance that is popular today

You know the kind; it says, "One man's religious belief is as good as that of any other." Carried to its logical conclusion, this means that Protestantism, Catholicism, Hinduism, Communism, and Father Divine-ism are all equally true. There is nothing to choose between them. If all religious opinions are of equal value, it can only mean that none of them is of any value. It means that we can know nothing about religion.

If we are going to think at all we must assume that we can come to conclusions and that some conclusions will have more to be said for them than others. Just because we cannot achieve final and absolute truth does not mean that we cannot know some truth. Where would we be in science and politics if we insisted that because we do not know everything, we must suppose that we know nothing and that one idea is as good as another?

If we believe that some truth, but not infallible truth, can be achieved, we will find in the debates of theology a healthy road to truth. We can find that our own position is strengthened by the criticism it receives from other positions. We may be led to abandon ideas that we come to see as false when they are under attack, or we may see a greater truth in them when we see how well they stand up under criticism. We must never forget that we can learn much from positions which, on the whole, we consider to be basically wrong. We can take it almost for granted that no position can hold the allegiance of sincere men if it has no truth whatsoever in it. As Reinhold Niebuhr says, many a truth has ridden into history on the back of an error. Lastly, we must remember that true tolerance does not say that there is no difference between conflicting views; it says that we will continue to respect and listen to a man even when we believe that he is wrong. True tolerance recognizes that a man has the right to be wrong and that even when he is most wrong he may have a truth that we do not have. A meaningful and creative discussion can be carried out in that spirit alone.

Despite the differences in theological thinking, there is a growing consensus of agreement in theological circles. Theology itself is seen as more vitally important than was the case thirty years ago. The fundamentalist-modernist controversy led many to feel that theology was a waste of time and a divider of Christians. We have come to see that we cannot face the modern world without a theological position upon which to stand. And we have seen that theology does not create our differences; it is one form in which they express themselves. The theological expression of our differences, however, enables us to understand their full implications, which is a prerequisite to overcoming them.

There is a renewed interest in the Bible that transcends all theological differences. This interest has led to great activity in the publishing of Bibles and books about the Bible in the last ten years. The Revised Standard Version of the Bible has broken all production records. *The Interpreter's Bible* is coming out as a far more ambitious series than anything that has been attempted for many years. There are several reasons for this concern with the Bible. The events of our century have broken down the optimism that man, by his unaided efforts, can solve all of his problems. To some this is a deplorable failure of nerve, and to others it is a realism that is a welcome relief from the naïveté of an earlier day. However we interpret it, this loss of optimism is a fact, and it is only natural that in light of it men should look again to the source of that movement which offers help to man from beyond himself.

Along with the resurgence of interest in the Bible, there is a growing realization of the differences between Christianity and other religions. We now realize that those who, a few years ago, pictured all of the world's religions as essentially similar, were oversimplifying the facts. We are learning that the price of tolerance is not necessarily the loss of our convictions. We can best express our love to the Hindu and others, not by pretending that basically we believe the same thing, but by honestly examining our differences and retaining respect and love for one another despite them. In this atmosphere we may both learn from and teach other religions.

A striking development of this century is that our theological differences no longer follow denominational lines. With the exception of some of the exclusively fundamentalist groups, practically all of our major denominations have representatives of every position I have treated here. In a particular denomination we may be somewhat more likely to find a particular type of theology, but in every case there are many exceptions. Theologically speaking, many a Christian finds himself closer to individuals in another denomination than to many members of his own denomination. The fundamentalist-modernist controversy split denominations (and even congregations) down the middle, and the diversity within denominations has continued. This is good evidence that it is not theology which is preserving the divisions of Protestantism.

It seems to me that there is today a tendency for theologians to search for a middle ground, and to find agreement apart from the extremes. The ecumenical movement has both resulted from and furthered this tendency. In such a situation, it is my opinion that the position of modern orthodoxy will grow in prominence. My cautious forecast would be that the immediate theological future lies with it. In making this forecast, I warn the reader that I am myself a follower of this school of thought, and the wish may be father to the prediction. It seems only fair, however, that I should reveal my own position so that the reader will beware of any bias or unfairness that has crept into my exposition of other schools of thought.

This book does not pretend to have been a complete or adequate treatment of modern Protestant theology. It has but one purpose: to stimulate the layman to read further and think more deeply about theological questions. It is meant to be the first step in a journey that will be fruitful and rewarding to the man who chooses to go further.

Suggestions for Further Reading

GENERAL BOOKS

Hughley, J. N., Trends in Protestant Social Idealism. 1948, King's Crown Press.

Soper, David W., Major Voices in American Theology. 1953, Westminster Press.

FUNDAMENTALISM

Carnell, Edward J., An Introduction to Christian Apologetics. 1948, William B. Eerdmans Publishing Company.

Machen, John G., What Is Faith? 1935, The Macmillan Company.

———, Christianity and Liberalism. 1923, The Macmillan Company.

Van Til, Cornelius, The New Modernism. 1946, Presbyterian and Reformed Publishing Company.

LIBERALISM

Bixler, Julius S., A Faith That Fulfills. 1951, Harper and Brothers.

Fosdick, Harry Emerson, As I See Religion. 1932, Harper and Brothers.

———, Rufus Jones Speaks to Our Time. 1951, The Macmillan Company.

McCown, Chester, The Search for the Real Jesus. 1940, Charles Scribner's Sons.

Mathews, Shailer, The Faith of Modernism. 1924, The Macmillan Company.

Waterman, Leroy, The Religion of Jesus. 1952, Harper and Brothers.

HUMANISM

Dewey, John, A Common Faith. 1934, Yale University Press.
Huxley, Julian, Religion Without Revelation. 1941, C. A. Watts & Co., Ltd.

NEO-LIBERALISM

Bennett, John, Christian Ethics and Social Policy. 1946, Charles Scribner's Sons.
———, Christianity and Communism. 1948, Haddam House.
———, Social Salvation. 1935, Charles Scribner's Sons.
Fosdick, Harry Emerson, The Man from Nazareth. 1949, Harper and Brothers.
Harkness, Georgia, Conflicts in Religious Thought. 1949, Harper and Brothers.
———, The Modern Rival of Christian Faith. 1952, Abingdon-Cokesbury Press.
Horton, Walter M., Realistic Theology. 1934, Harper and Brothers.
Trueblood, Elton, The Predicament of Modern Man. 1944, Harper and Brothers.
———, Foundations for Reconstruction. 1946, Harper and Brothers.
———, Alternative to Futility. 1948, Harper and Brothers.

NEO-ORTHODOXY

Brunner, Emil, The Divine-Human Encounter. 1943, Westminster Press.
———, The Scandal of Christianity. 1951, Westminster Press.
Hubben, William, Four Prophets of Our Destiny. 1952, The Macmillan Company.

NEO-ORTHODOXY (NIEBUHR)

Niebuhr, Reinhold, The Children of Light and the Children of Darkness. 1944, Charles Scribner's Sons.

———, Christian Realism and Political Problems. 1953, Charles Scribner's Sons.

———, An Interpretation of Christian Ethics. 1935, Harper and Brothers.

Davies, David R., Reinhold Niebuhr: Prophet from America. 1945, The Macmillan Company.

———, On to Orthodoxy. 1949, The Macmillan Company.

TILLICH

Tillich, Paul, Love, Power, and Justice. 1954, Oxford University Press.

———, The Shaking of the Foundations. 1948, Charles Scribner's Sons.

ORTHODOXY AS A GROWING TRADITION

Baillie, Donald M., God Was in Christ. 1948, Charles Scribner's Sons.

Butterfield, Herbert, Christianity and History. 1950, Charles Scribner's Sons.

Lewis, C. S., Mere Christianity. 1952, The Macmillan Company.

———, Miracles. 1947, The Macmillan Company.

Stewart, James S., A Faith to Proclaim. 1953, Charles Scribner's Sons.

Walsh, Chad, Stop Looking and Listen. 1947, Harper and Brothers.

Whale, John S., Christian Doctrine. 1941, The Macmillan Company.

Index

Index